Tha

Jarrold Publishing

CONTENTS

Introducing Thailand	3
Essential details in brief	7
A land between agriculture and industry	8
Some special features	10
Buddha and Nirvana	13
The Thai language	15
Signposts of history	16
Phases of history	17
Holy days and holidays	20
Sport in Thailand	21
Food and drink: Thai specialities	23
Shopping – the great temptation	26
Wai and wat	28
Other customs: a brief etiquette	29
Hints for your holiday	31
Where to go and what to see	32
Bangkok	32
Across the Great Plain	48
The coastal resorts on the Gulf of Thailand	55
The north-east: a journey into the Khmer age	62
Central Thailand	69
Chiang Mai and the north	73
The long tail: the south of Thailand	84
Useful things to know	92
Index	95
Maps	
Bangkok	34/35
West and north-west of Bangkok	51
The coastal resorts on the Gulf of Thailand	61
The north-east of Thailand	67
The area around Sukhothai	71
Chiang Mai	75
The north of Thailand	79
The east coast of the Malayan Peninsula	86
The south of Thailand	89
General map	back cover

Title page: Traditional Thai dancers, Bangkok

A spirit house (left) on one of Thailand's waterways

Introducing Thailand

You will probably first set foot on Thai soil at the kingdom's Don Muang airport – and you will be amazed. You will be standing in a gigantic, ultra-modern, air-conditioned cathedral made of glass and teak and invisible reinforced concrete, and there will be nothing to indicate that you have just landed in the middle of the tropics or, more precisely, in the Land of Smiles. But the uniformed guards in their little glass booths will not be the smiling sort. In their freshly pressed clothes, they will thumb through their Wanted Persons file before finally stamping your passport.

You see to your luggage, change your money and get your first fistful of baht, order a taxi – which you pay for at the counter – and only then comes the big shock. Between March and September above all, it hits you immediately you leave the cool arrival lounge and find yourself standing close to the Equator: the heat of the tropics! As long as you are travelling in Thailand, you will never escape it – whether you are on the beach at Phuket, in the mountain forests above Chiang Mai, or in the ruins at Sukhothai – not even at midnight. You may possibly find it cooler about an hour before sunrise, near the sea. And of course in air-conditioned hotels, shopping centres, banks, and the better class of taxi.

From the airport it is 22 km to the centre of Bangkok – only half an hour, or maybe an hour, but time enough for a first surprising glimpse of this holiday paradise. What was that flashing past? Warehouses, factories, blocks of flats, a palm tree, another

Thai girls, Chiang Mai

palm tree, buses, more buses, strange architecture, a few small, well-polished cars, adverts like the ones at home, the golden tip of a temple, more and more high-rise hotels, towering office-blocks, traffic lights changing every minute, pith helmets, snow-white, flower-clad dolls' houses on stilts, signs you cannot read – an absolute flood of fresh images, noises and smells as you approach an American/Japanese/European metropolis. Bangkok, Thailand, South-East Asia. After an exhausting trip, you have finally arrived.

The Land of Smiles

If there really is a land of smiles anywhere in the world, then Thailand must be it. Buddha smiles, in gold, stone, and gems. The dancing girls smile. The policemen smile. The monks smile. Only the temple demons bare their teeth at you as if about to bite – but they look so friendly that you actually feel like stroking them.

In other parts of Asia, foreigners quicken their step when passing a group of locals in a deserted part of town. But not here. It is rare to find any criminal activity in Thailand, even in the capital. Women travelling alone here are favourably impressed. Sitting in a splendid, air-conditioned taxi and travelling through Bangkok's chaotic traffic, you see children looking out of the trundling buses and waving at you. They are simply happy that you have come as a stranger to their land, and that you are clearly having a much better, cooler time than they are. Smiling young people constantly approach you and ask politely how you are. Is it a trick of some sort? Are you going to be conned into buying some over-priced rubbish? No. These people are friendly because that is their nature. Strangers are treated graciously. People smile at them. So smile back!

The many and varied faces of Thailand

A prosperous, orderly, friendly, hard-working country – that is often Thailand's image. But is it in fact prosperous? The per capita income has trebled over the last fifteen years and is far in excess of that of other parts of Indo-China; but it cannot be compared with the figures for the wealthy nations of Europe – far from it. Still, nobody goes hungry in Thailand. Bangkok is a modern business metropolis with everything that entails: luxury living, chain stores, problems with drinking-water and sewage, too many cars, large numbers of immigrants, a television and a fridge in every house, and a domestic electricity supply. The supermarkets are full, the restaurants are full, and there is a full range of entertainments. There is also a full complement of police and of the unemployed.

Thailand is a pious nation. Young men with shaven heads, wrapped in the saffron robes of Buddhist monks, walk the land with measured tread. In many places, temples are the only real sights worth seeing – even the smallest village is crowned by the gilded spire of a little temple.

The real power in Thailand is exercised by the army. You see uniforms everywhere, a confusing welter of them. They are always spick and span: knife-edge creases, starched shirts, polished helmets. It is an extremely orderly country. If anyone makes an important decision, it is nearly always a general. Sometimes you might think that even the temples and the museums are occupied by the army. But you would be wrong; it is just that the guards wear uniforms.

Fishermen after work

Thailand lies between the 6th and the 21st parallels, level with Sudan, and is very hot. The country's last remaining tigers are still at large, roaming the jungles of the north. Elephants drag great teak-trees down to the waterways. On the gleaming white beaches of the south you will hear the roar of the South China Sea. You are in a land that can truly be called exotic. Three hundred different varieties of butterfly flutter around Thailand, and a thousand different orchids blossom. There are also about forty different sorts of snake, but don't let that put you off!

The visitor to Thailand

What are you expecting from Thailand? The sun, the tropics, the Orient, beaches, service, all sorts of delicacies? It certainly offers all that. The country's tourist infrastructure is exemplary, the restaurants offer quite superb food, the made-to-measure tailors work away like demons, the prices are very attractive to the average European. Everything is designed to give you a flawless holiday – sunlit, relatively inexpensive, and unforgettable.

The kingdom of Thailand may be ancient, but as a tourist destination the country is still in its infancy. It was discovered by the Americans during the Vietnam War, in the 1960s. They used to send their soldiers over to Bangkok or to the dreamy beaches on the Gulf of Thailand to give them a week's holiday where they could forget the war. In doing so, they discovered and created Pattaya, Thailand's leading resort.

Thirty years ago, Thailand was beyond the reach of the average European's budget. Three things were generally known about it: that it used to be known as Siam, that such things as Siamese cats and Siamese twins existed, and that Yul Brynner played the King of Siam in the film of a musical. Later, people began to see in magazines or on television pictures of a fabulously beautiful queen and her tranquil king. The king and queen are still there, and are called Bhumibol and Sirikit. In December 1987, the whole of Thailand celebrated the King's birthday, his sixtieth, with rapturous exuberance. Traces of the splendid festivities can still be seen: the main temple at Wat Phra Keo was newly gilded for the occasion, and now glistens just as it must have done on the day it was opened. Pictures of the highly revered and highly educated King (whom, incidentally, visitors should *never* openly criticise) hang in every living room, in every shop, in every office – and even in brothels.

Of course Thailand has its problems – severe pollution, the wanton destruction of its northern forests, the influx of refugees from Vietnam and Cambodia. But for the average holidaymaker, it still represents the exotic East. If you want to immerse yourself in the Orient, but would nevertheless like to spend the late afternoon in some cool hotel with an ice-cold gin and tonic; if you want to explore the tropical Far East, without the risk of being attacked by political rebels; if you want to observe mysterious and splendid rites; if you like things to be strange, but at the same time comfortable; and if you want to experience the atmosphere of a major Asian metropolis, without being confronted wherever you go by depressing wretchedness – then you will feel very much at home in Thailand.

The beach at Pattaya

Essential details in brief

Thai dancers

Name:	Muang T'ai or Prathet T'ai (Land of the Free).
Form of government:	Constitutional monarchy (since 1932).
Head of state:	King Bhumibol Adulyadej (Rama IX), b. 1927.
Size:	514,000 sq km.
Population:	About 50 million.
Capital:	Bangkok (officially Phra Nakhon Krung Thep – 'City of Angels').
Religions:	95% Buddhist, 4% Muslim, 0.5% Christian.
Ethnic blend:	80% Thai, 10% Chinese, 4% Malay, 6% other.
Population density:	98 people per sq km.
Life expectancy:	63 years.
Doctors:	One per 8,220 of population.
Flag:	Red-white-blue-white-red in horizontal stripes.
Main exports:	Rice, tapioca, maize, rubber, tin, textiles.
Currency:	One baht = 100 satang.
Work-force:	67% in agriculture, 21% in service sector, 12% in industry.
Main trading partners:	Japan, USA, Germany, Britain, Singapore, Hong Kong, Indonesia.

Rice is harvested several times a year

A land between agriculture and industry

Right at the end of Thailand's list of economic statistics there is a sparkling little figure: it exports 11 million carats of gemstones each year – rubies, sapphires, emeralds and other glittering treasures. It also sells seemingly innumerable bales of its famous shimmering, colourful silks to foreign customers: 238,000 sq m each year. How nice to travel to such a wealthy country!

But unfortunately there are other statistics too. There is an annual budget deficit of billions of dollars, and the population is growing by over 2% a year. What does 2.2% matter? The answer is: a great deal. It means that within the next thirty-five years the population will double, from about 50 million to about 100 million. (At the end of the Second World War there were fewer than 20 million people living in Thailand.) It is only in recent years that population growth has been slowed by means of educational programmes. Today, the rate lies well below that of the average developing nation, and Thailand is proud of this achievement.

The majority of Thais are employed in the agricultural sector. This is how the visitor really likes to photograph them: steering their phlegmatic water buffaloes through the fields, riding on elephants which drag mighty teak boles, or at home in their shaded huts, patient tenant farmers smiling under their airy straw hats; all apparently impervious to the communist revolution which, since the end of the Vietnam War, has spread ever closer to Thailand.

A land between agriculture and industry

Nobody goes hungry. Flying into Bangkok, you see regular-shaped ponds glinting in the sunlight: the nation's rice-fields. These are Thailand's real wealth, providing a harvest of 14 million tonnes each year, and comprising the country's major export item. And yet experts are worried that the yield per hectare is not increasing, but rather diminishing. For years farmers managed simply by chopping down fresh areas of forest and ploughing the land to make more rice-fields. This is how Thailand became one of the world's leading exporters of rice; but the country needs increasing quantities of it to feed its own growing population.

Thailand produces an annual 7 million tonnes of tapioca or cassava (the tropical equivalent of potatoes), the same quantity of cane sugar, 5 million tonnes each of maize and rubber, and in addition tobacco and millet, cotton, sesame, coconuts and jute. Further tropical products include kenaf, kapok, mung, and castor, otherwise known as *ricinus communis*. Thailand is a major producer of castor oil, which nowadays is used almost exclusively for industrial purposes – to make lubricants, and in the soap industry. However, these rather splendid statistics can be deceptive. In some areas, the export trade has faltered; an example is tapioca. Thirty years ago, this nourishing tuber was unknown in Thailand. Suddenly the world market began to cry out for it, especially as an ingredient for concentrated foodstuffs produced in Europe. Great numbers of Thai farmers immediately switched to growing tapioca – indeed, far too many. The price fell and fell, and a lot of the growers were bankrupted.

Yet Thailand has a very favourable location: Singapore, Hong Kong, Taiwan and Japan all compete to buy the fruits of the Thai harvest. Japan has long since taken over from the USA, which for years was Thailand's main customer.

In Asian terms, Thailand is a wealthy country, but it lacks a number of elements which would make it more economically secure: oil, coal and iron. There is a shortage of energy, so it is fortunate that the Thais have found natural gas in the Gulf of Thailand. Irrigation is also not without its problems. The local microclimate has been badly damaged by the slashing and burning of forests. Bangkok is expanding into a major industrial conglomeration, and is faced with all the problems associated with an explosive rate of growth. Deep-sea fishing in the gulf is being badly affected by corrosive discharges pumped into the sea by the Menam River – as well as by reckless levels of fishing.

But alongside growing problems and growing debts, prosperity is also increasing. Thailand is blessed with tin deposits, and also mines zinc and lead, wolfram, copper and felspar. And 30% of the country is covered by forest. This is not all high-quality teak, however. Since Thailand only produces a little lignite, a cheap supply of wood is needed for burning in the nation's cooking stoves. Moreover, the demand for teak, with its very hard, resistant qualities, is very much subject to the current fashions in furniture in other countries, and demand is falling. Nevertheless, Thailand still produces 250,000 cu m of teak each year.

Modern economies can only function properly if supported by an efficient infrastructure. The latter is expensive, requiring high levels of investment. Japan in particular pumps vast sums into what it sees as a politically stable country, and has become Thailand's largest creditor. The Thai currency is one of the most solid in all Asia, and is coupled with the dollar. If the dollar rises, so does the baht.

International experts think that in the next ten years Thailand has a good chance of joining the 'Young Tigers Club', consisting of Taiwan, South Korea, Hong Kong and Singapore, and of crossing the threshold from developing nation to industrial nation. For example, cars are already being assembled and microchips manufactured on behalf of Japanese companies. There are still, of course, huge gaps in the country's road system, particularly in the northern provinces. The railway system, taken as a whole, extends to a mere 4,000 km. By contrast, the ancient waterways – both rivers and canals – are over twice as long, almost 10,000 km in all.

Tourism naturally features among the many branches of the national economy. When you see all the Japanese, Germans, Americans, French and Australians crowding into Bangkok airport, you will quite innocently assume that like you they are contributing to the well-being of Thailand. But there are now studies which seriously question that assumption: the income from tourism, you will read, largely flows into the coffers of foreign investors.

Some special features
Little 'bird cages' for demons

You will notice the little toy houses on your very first day. They sit head-high on pillars, columns, and trestles, and are called *samprapoms* – spirit houses. Anyone building a house in Thailand builds another one at the same time for the spirit who lives on that piece of land and who might be displaced by the new building. The spirit might otherwise seek revenge. This is the way to appease him – with a little house on a pillar. It is vital that the shadow of the big house never falls across the spirit house. What is more, the spirit must be pampered every day with gifts – rice, flowers, incense and fruit. These spirit houses have nothing at all to do with Buddhism; they stem from pre-Buddhist times.

Sometimes there is a spirit house standing next to a blind bend in the road, as a road safety measure. If an evil spirit can live in a nice little house, then he will not hang about in the road endangering motorists' lives – so the theory goes.

Samprapom and house

Buddhist monks in Nakhon Pathom

'Temporary' monks

There are about 300,000 Buddhist monks wending their silent way through Thailand, and they are immediately recognisable by their saffron-yellow robes. They shave their heads and walk barefoot. They gather their food in black bowls, and anyone who approaches one of these monks and puts food in his bowl is considered lucky. The monks offer no thanks. Quite the opposite: those giving alms bow in gratitude. The monks live in monasteries, or *wats*, and only one in three will remain a monk throughout his life. The majority serve on a temporary basis, for between a week and several years. Every pious Thai male undertakes at least once in his life to lead the life of the yellow-clad mendicant – in order to come closer to the Buddhist ideal. The monks live almost entirely without possessions: they are only allowed a razor, a parasol and a piece of cloth. They strain everything they drink through the cloth, to avoid swallowing any live insects. They are allowed to eat meat and also to smoke, but handling money, even the smallest amounts, is an offence against their rules. The ones dressed in white are not monks: they are nuns. It takes a second glance to verify the fact.

A delicacy for the brave

Whether you are in a bus, in a taxi, or on the street, between the months of April and August you are likely to notice a powerful and very unpleasant smell. It comes from Thailand's great summer delicacy, the durian fruit; its full botanical name is *durio zibethinus*, but it is more commonly known as the stink-fruit. The fruit is green, has quite harmless thorns as thick as your finger and a stalk that looks like a cooking spoon, and grows to be bigger than a man's head, weighing up to 4 kg. Underneath the extremely thick skin are large cream-coloured kernels – the part you actually eat. The stench is ghastly, but the taste is incomparable – a mixture of cream, nuts, and soft cheese. Durian is expensive, especially out of season. It is above all men who swear by it: eating it is said to have a dramatic effect on their virility.

Thai silk

After the Second World War, an American called Jim Thompson decided to settle in Bangkok, having worked for the previous few years as a secret agent. He started up an organisation for buying and selling Thai silk. He had new colours produced – glowing reds, a sumptuous range of greens, and every possible shade of blue. He adapted the quality, the colours, the patterns and the various weaves to the demands of the American market. Suddenly Thai silk was all the rage and Jim Thompson became a rich man. At his house he collected outstanding works of Thai art, showing unerring taste. In 1967 he visited Malaysia, which at that time was threatened by communist terrorists. One day he happened to leave the house where he was staying, and he has never been seen since. You can visit his house in Bangkok; it is actually made up of parts taken from seven houses from various places in Thailand. And his business, Jim Thompson Thai Silk, still exists at 9 Suriwonose Road. The silks are a bit expensive, but their quality is unequalled.

Thirty thousand hammer-blows

In Thailand's temples you can buy pieces of wafer-thin gold leaf, about the size of postage stamps. Stick them on to any Buddha figure and you have done a good

Working elephants

deed on your path to eternity. This gold leaf is produced by age-old methods: a nugget the size of a tiny pebble is beaten with a heavy bronze hammer. Some 30,000 blows later, the nugget has been turned into 1 sq m of filmy gold. Top workers in this gold-hammering trade are paid about three times as much as a school-teacher makes.

The cleverest bulldozers in the world

Fifty years ago, elephants were as common a sight on the streets of Siam as horses were in some parts of Europe. Cars have since displaced both. Only in the teak forests of northern Thailand does the elephant, massively strong but also good-natured and intelligent, still do sterling service. The terrain is often so difficult and the work so intricate that bulldozers could never replace them. Elephants do not need access roads cut out of the jungle; they do not need fuel depots; and they do not need any special maintenance. True, they can only work for five hours a day before stopping to go for a swim or to search the jungle for food. They are timid creatures, but are quickly reassured by the voices of their drivers, or *mahouts*. The elephant and its driver will more often than not grow up together.

Buddha and Nirvana

Out of every 100 Thais, 95 are Buddhists. In the temples Buddha can be seen sitting, standing, walking, or lying down. He smiles with his eyes fixed on the ground, and those who understand such things may read from the individual gesture of his hands what is preoccupying him. If the hand is hanging limply, this signifies fearlessness; if the arm is pointing upwards but the fingers remain horizontal, this signifies veneration; if the hand hangs down with the fingers spread, this is an unmistakable sign of his compassion.

Every Thai male is supposed to become a monk at least once in his life. Even King Bhumibol once changed his regal garments for the yellow robes of the monk.

Ancient Siam to some extent adjusted the doctrine of Buddha to accommodate its own beliefs, allowing in a whole host of spirits and demons; these must be shown respect if they are to ward off illness, poverty, deceit, and traffic accidents. The

Thai Buddhists at prayer

Buddha and Nirvana

Buddhist doctrine is drawn on a large scale, and for those rooted in Christianity it tends to be a closed book. The most surprising aspect of the Buddhist philosophy is that it does without a god and without eternal life. Its highest goal is not some kind of heaven where all is blissfully happy; the Buddhist doctrine strives towards nothingness.

Buddha was a prince called Siddhartha, born in about 560 BC in the foothills of the Himalayas. His father was a king or prince, and the boy was not only spoilt but discontented with his lot. At the age of about twenty-nine he left the kingdom, abandoning his princess, his family, his riches, his friends, his palace, and his gardens. He led the life of a wandering pilgrim, fasting, contemplating, chastening himself, and helping the sick and the poor. At long last, while sitting under a fig tree, he received enlightenment. All of this took place in India, 2,500 years ago.

Buddha instructs us that life ends in death and is followed by rebirth; since every new life is burdened with fresh suffering, there can truly be nothing more beautiful than once and for all to reach the end — and not to be reborn. This end is nothingness, or Nirvana. It is reached by adhering strictly to the rules Buddha himself followed: dispensing with all desires, possessions, power, actions and pleasures frees man from suffering. The 'eightfold path' towards the achievement of Nirvana includes the disciplines of right speech, right action and right meditation.

The Buddhist doctrine is complicated. It not only demands poverty and virtue, but frequently prescribes rather tortuous avenues of thought, all of which are more philosophical than religious. It recommends four 'noble truths'. Compared with Christianity and its doctrine of divine salvation, Buddhism is not really a religion, but is more like a doctrine of how to attain wisdom. It is absolutely certain that Buddha did not strive to found a religion: he simply wanted to be a gentle and pious reformer. Buddhism remains to this day a very tolerant faith. It has never pursued other faiths with fire and sword.

Apart from those who remain monks for life, Buddhists are not organised into a strict religious community. There are no bishops, although there are abbots, and there is a patriarch appointed by the King. Charity is given on a grand scale, but in an unstructured manner. The ethical rules are short and to the point: one must not kill, nor steal, nor lie, nor lead an unchaste life, nor take intoxicating substances.

By contrast, life in the 25,000 or so Thai monasteries is complicated and strict, with precisely ordained readings from holy scriptures and with difficult meditation exercises. What often appears to the outsider to be an ingredient of Buddhism usually has nothing to do with Buddhist doctrine. The existence of the little spirit houses is a product of simple superstition. The cremation of the dead is a purely worldly rite, for Buddha never worried about what should be done with a dead body. For him, it was wholly unimportant. Even pilgrimages to revered shrines and holy places do not appear in the pure form of the doctrine. And what of the famous footprint made by Buddha at Saraburi? Of course it is not genuine, since the Enlightened One never went near Saraburi, and everyone knows as much. But the journey there is taxing, a sacrifice, and thus a small step on the path towards self-renunciation.

Buddha not only dominates temples and houses in Thailand, he also forms the principal motif in the art of ancient Siam. No king has ever been portrayed — only Buddha.

The Thai language

If you are a man and want to say 'I' in the Thai language, then you must say *phom*. If you are a woman, then 'I' becomes *dichan*. The Thai alphabet has three letters for the sound 's', four for 'k', and eight for 't'. Words which transcribed into roman characters look like 'mai' or 'kao' are capable of being spoken in such differing ways in Thai that they can mean the most diverse things, depending on whether you drop your voice, or start in a deep voice, or give it a slight lilt, or speak in a high tone. *Mai* can mean 'new', 'burn', 'no', or a certain type of question. It is possible to utter the *kao* syllable in a deep voice, a mid-range voice, or a high voice, or in a falling or a rising tone, and to make the 'ao' part long or short. The meanings then range from 'rice' to 'mountain', taking in 'nine', 'old', 'knee', 'step', 'glue', 'white', 'news', and 'the smell of fish'.

In addition, there are three major dialect regions in Thailand: the north, the north-east, and the south. Each of these dialects, moreover, has its own tonal system. However, a standard Thai – Siamese – is taught in all schools. It is the official language, as spoken in Bangkok. It does have its plus side, too: the grammar is very simple. The written language does have about seventy letters, but is very beautiful, and it runs, like ours, from left to right.

If you are aiming to transact important business in Thailand you should also learn Chinese, for this is the written language of the business world. Chu, and not Mandarin, is the version used. In court circles, however, neither Thai nor Chu is of any use at all. The King and the highest-ranking princes only converse in Rajasap, a court language just about comparable with ecclesiastical Latin.

The transliteration of Thai words into roman characters does not really indicate their true pronunciation. But the difficulties faced by the Thais when trying to pronounce European languages are even greater. As a rule 'l' and 'r' are mixed up, and this will turn 'grill' into 'glirr', or 'living room' into 'riving loom'. The Hilton Hotel sounds like the 'hintan' – and that is how it is known to the great majority of taxi-drivers.

But if you really want to learn a useful word, then learn *sawadie* – the standard greeting at all times of day and night. However, there is one little oddity: women say *sawadie kha*, whilst men say *sawadie khrab*.

Warding off evil spirits in an Akha village

Signposts of history

1st–6th c. AD: The Mon, culturally influenced by India, establish various states in Thailand.

7th c: Buddhist Dvaravati kingdom of the Mon on the Menam River.

8th–12th c: The Khmer from Cambodia extend their empire and oust the Mon. The Thais migrate here from Yunnan Province, China.

13th c: The advance of the Thais breaks Khmer dominion. Thai principalities are created in northern Thailand. The Thais found the Sukhothai kingdom. After the death of King Rama Khamheng, the kingdom wanes.

14th c: Founding of the Ayuthaya kingdom (kingdom of Siam) around 1350 by King Ramathibodi I.

15th c: Struggles among the northern Thai principalities, and between them and the Ayuthaya kingdom.

16th c: First links with Europe. Repeated incursions by the Burmese. Ayuthaya conquered in 1569. At the end of the 16th c., Ayuthaya is liberated and united with the principality of Chiang Mai.

17th c: First trading links with Europe.

18th c: Renewed Burmese incursions; they destroy Ayuthaya in 1767. General Taksin drives out the Burmese.

1792: As King Rama I, General Phya Chakri ascends the throne. Bangkok becomes the capital.

19th c: King Mongkut and King Chulalongkorn conclude trade agreements with European nations, and reform the administration and the military along European lines. These progressive developments and the people's national pride (together with British/French rivalry) help Siam to remain independent of the colonial powers.

20th c: Under *Entente* pressure, Siam enters the First World War in 1917 on the side of the Allies.

1932: Coup d'état. Absolutist monarchy converted to constitutional monarchy.

1936: Phibul Songkram becomes prime minister, and rules like a dictator. In 1939, Siam is renamed Thailand. In the Second World War, Phibul allies Thailand with Japan. He resigns when the outcome of the war becomes inevitable. After 1945, the royal house distances itself from Phibul's policies. Thailand becomes an ally of the USA.

1946: Following the murder of his brother, Bhumibol ascends the throne as King Rama IX. The military are the vital factor in domestic politics.

1948–57: Phibul once again prime minister.

1957–63: Sarit Thanarat, chief of the armed forces, consolidates political stability and initiates new economic development.

1963–73: Kittikachorn prime minister. Bloody suppression of student unrest, with several hundred deaths. Kittikachorn exiled.

1973–76: Short-lived cabinets. Renewed student unrest.

1977: General Kriangsak prime minister. In 1980, and again in 1986, General Prem Tinsulanonda prime minister. Trade unions permitted. Democratic reforms; a measure of liberalisation.

July 1988: Fresh elections. Chatichai Choonhavan succeeds Prem as prime minister.

1991: Choonhavan's government toppled by bloodless military coup in February. Fresh elections promised; interim government appointed in March.

Phases of history

Of all the many Thai rulers, only one has become famous in the West: King Mongkut. He owes his fame to Hollywood, which on two occasions has filmed an episode from Siamese history in which an English schoolmistress arrives at the royal court, tutors the young princes, and causes a great deal of confusion. The first film was called *Anna and the King of Siam* and the second was *The King and I*; in 1988 a third version was filmed – partly in Thailand itself.

King Mongkut reigned from 1851 to 1868. He has another name, which makes him easier to place: Rama IV. All the kings of the Chakri dynasty, which is still in power, have been called Rama, with the appropriate number. The history of modern Siam begins around 1800 with King Rama I. Later Ramas did away with Bangkok's draconian court etiquette, which made the notoriously strict ceremonial at the Spanish court seem lax. For example, anyone who whispered to his neighbour – perhaps a soldier of the palace guard or a servant – whilst in the royal audience-chamber was beheaded. The same fate might be expected if one happened to touch the king, the queen, or one of the princes.

If the king was going up the Menam River on his ceremonial barque, nobody was allowed to approach his vessel. If the unthinkable did indeed happen, and the royal barque was made to rock, there was only one outcome: a cry of 'off with his head!' There was a reason for all this: the royal house was attempting to protect itself from would-be assassins. The unusually strict court etiquette did, it must be said, lead to one particular tragedy which played a large part in the eventual abolishing of the old ceremonials. The wife of Rama V was being rowed along in her boat when it tipped over. The servants were able to swim, but the Queen could not. However, the servants did not rescue the Queen – court etiquette forbade them to touch their mistress.

The Thais conquer Thailand

The Thai people have a history stretching back perhaps more than 4,000 years. Very few documents from the middle period have survived, and none at all from the earliest period. The Thais come from the south of China, and are in fact closely related to the southern Chinese. Gradually, Thai tribes migrated further south and south-west, until in 1250 the Mongols invaded the old Thai homeland. The Thais fled to what is now northern Thailand, and there they came across their own advance guard, as it were, who had already intermingled to a certain extent with peoples such as the Lawa.

A time of more war than peace

The Thais proceeded to establish their first capital, Sukhothai. They advanced as far as Malaya, and soon came to rule over the major part of the peninsula of Indo-China, from the Mekong to Petchaburi. The capital was switched from Sukhothai to Munang Nakhon Sawan, then to Kamphaeng Phet, and then Suvarnabhumi. During this period, the Thais swallowed up more Indo-Chinese principalities, with apparently insatiable greed. In 1350, they founded another new capital: Ayuthaya. Even if your visit to Thailand is only brief, you should note the name, and go there: it is only an hour and a half from Bangkok by car. The new Ayuthaya kingdom was powerful. It developed its own unmistakable art forms, and Theravada Buddhism took root throughout the population. However, it was rather more aggressive activities that sustained its power. Fertile areas of land were taken from the Thais' neighbours, the Cambodian Khmer, and villages were burnt to the ground. The Thais also destroyed the Cambodian capital, Angkor. They plundered treasures from its temples and carried off 90,000 prisoners, who were never returned. For 400 years, the smiling Thais were feared in South-East Asia. Relations with arch-enemies such as Cambodia (now Kampuchea) have not been entirely healed to this day.

What the Thais did to the people of Laos and Kampuchea they had to suffer themselves at the hands of their deadly enemies the Burmese. Around 1555 the Burmese subjugated almost the whole of Siam, raping and oppressing as they went, burning temples, and crushing the Thai state. But it was not long before there emerged a national hero, Phra Naret, who reconquered everything around him and exacted dire revenge.

First contacts with Europe

During the 17th c. the first Europeans (Portuguese) began to trickle into Indo-China: seafarers and spice-traders, even the odd zealous missionary armed with his crucifix. One Greek adventurer even rose to become one of the king's ministers. This was during the reign of the Sun King in France, and the Greek managed to persuade his exotic king, Phra Narai, to send a delegation of unparalleled splendour to Versailles. Louis XIV was quite overcome by the magnificence of the smiling ambassadors, who aroused his acquisitive instincts towards their country. But nothing came of his desire. In fact, Siam was one of the few overseas countries to be spared the rapacious activities of European imperialists. Unlike all of its neighbours, which were 'collected' and plundered by the English, the French, and the Dutch, it was never made a colony. The Thai are proud to translate their name for you: 'The Free'.

The era of the Chakri dynasty

The various Thai principalities fought and mauled each other in a series of civil wars throughout the 18th c. The Burmese exploited this situation to launch repeated attacks on the country. For two whole years they besieged the magnificent capital, Ayuthaya, and eventually took the city in 1767. The ruins can still be seen today, and form one of the most magnificent sights in Thailand. Once the capital had fallen, General Taksin gathered together the remains of the defeated army, re-equipped his soldiers, and sent them out again into battle. He had no intention of rebuilding the pile of rubble which had once been Ayuthaya. He wanted a new capital. He declared himself king, and as the site of the new capital he selected Thonburi on the Menam River. Today it is a suburb of Bangkok.

The victorious King Taksin did not rule for long. His piety turned to religious mania, and he was eventually killed by a group of generals and ministers.

Next to rule was another general, Phya Chakri. He made Bangkok the capital of Siam and himself its king: Rama I. Rama V, King Chulalongkorn, whose name crops up in any account of modern Siam, played a vastly significant role. He ruled the country for forty-two years, from 1868 to 1910, abolishing slavery, establishing the

Wat Mahatat, Ayuthaya

kingdom's first school system, and creating the first network of roads. His tremendous achievements may be summarised very simply: he put an end to the Middle Ages in Siam. He travelled throughout Europe and on his return presented to Siam, as a kind of souvenir, something absolutely novel: the country's first hospital. Reluctantly, but with great shrewdness, he ceded 100,000 sq km of territory, including the whole of Laos, to the predatory England and France; this manoeuvre meant that Siam remained a free country – and it is still free today. King Bhumibol, born in 1927, is the ninth ruler of the Chakri dynasty, and is thus known as Rama IX.

Absolutist monarchy came to an end in the summer of 1932. Since then, Thailand has been a constitutional monarchy: the king is head of state, but power rests in the government. In practice, this meant the generals in the 1960s and 1970s. In the modern part of Bangkok there is a monument to democracy, on the site of the October 1973 student demonstrations pressing for change. There were bloody exchanges on the streets. Prime Minister Kittikachorn was forced to resign, and King Bhumibol appointed a civilian government, which was toppled in October 1976 by a military coup. The military nominated a civilian government, but themselves took over just a year later. Thailand has been attempting to restore democracy since 1978. General Prem Tinsulanonda became prime minister, but in 1981 and 1985 had to survive coup attempts. He ruled with an iron fist until he voluntarily handed over to a civilian, Chatichai Choonhavan, in 1988. In February 1991 Choonhavan was toppled by a bloodless military coup. The junta, led by General Sunthorn, promised fresh elections within six months, and in March an interim government was appointed. The essentially muted response to the coup, at home and abroad, reflected the non-violent nature of its execution.

Holy days and holidays

Phra-Buddhabaht Festival (end of January/beginning of February): The Buddhist faithful make a pilgrimage to 'Buddha's holy footprint' near the mountain temple of Saraburi (136 km from Bangkok). Festival in the temple, traditional music and other performances, bazaar.

Kite Season (February to April): Competitions with all shapes, sizes, and colours of kites, weekday afternoons, on the Pra Mane Ground in front of Wat Phra Keo, Bangkok.

Chiang Mai Flower Carnival (around the second week of February, when most flowers are in blossom): Processions, exhibitions of tropical flowers and orchids.

Maha Bucha (February): This festival commemorates the day when Buddha elaborated the foundations of his doctrine. Evening processions around the temples, with lighted candles. (Statutory holiday.)

Songkran (April 13th–15th): The traditional Thai New Year celebration, a joyous popular festival in which Buddha figures, monks, and the people themselves are sprayed with water. Fish and birds are released. At its most beautiful in Chiang Mai. (Statutory holiday.)

Royal Ploughing Ceremony (May): A colourful procession of Brahmin priests – the festival is of Hindu origin – files in front of the Grand Palace in Bangkok. A ritual furrow is drawn with a gilded plough, and from the behaviour of the water buffaloes the priests divine the yield of the forthcoming harvest. Grains of rice blessed by the monks are distributed to the farmers. The King attends the ceremony. (Statutory holiday.)

The Rocket Festival (last week of May – after the harvest and before the rains): Parades, dances, and a great deal of music. As a finale, rockets are fired into the air.

Visakha Bucha (during full moon in May): To commemorate Buddha's birth, his enlightenment, and his gaining Nirvana. Temples are ornamented with flowers and lanterns. Candlelit processions around the temples. Thailand's most holy festival. (Statutory holiday.)

Asalha Bucha (July; the eve of the Buddhist three-month fast): On this day, all monks return to their temples to meditate and to give instruction during the period of fasting, which coincides with the rainy season.

The Queen's Birthday (August 12th): The Queen takes part in religious ceremonials and distributes gifts to monks. (Statutory holiday.)

Loi Krathong (during full moon in November): Little vessels made of lotus leaves are floated on the lakes and rivers, filled with flowers, incense sticks, and lighted candles. The festival gives thanks to Mae Knongkha, the goddess of the waters.

The Surin Elephant Festival (third weekend in November): Huge elephant 'round-up', featuring races and demonstrations. A brilliantly colourful popular festival with various competitions.

The King's Birthday and the Thai National Day (December 5th): Parades throughout the country. In the evening, houses are decorated with coloured lights. (Statutory holiday.)

Golf on one of the excellent courses

Sport in Thailand

For tourists
Swimming is the top holiday sport in a country with 2,000 km of coast — although only a small proportion of the coast has actually been opened up for tourists.
Diving: Diving establishments have been set up in Pattaya, whilst in Phuket there is a diving base with a motorboat and all the necessary equipment.
Waterskiing and parasailing are offered in the main resorts of Pattaya and Phuket. Near Bangkok there are two further waterskiing centres, both on the Chao-Phraya River.
Raft trips down the River Kwai and the Nam Mae Kok provide the opportunity for a close encounter with the natural world of Thailand.
Golf: alongside a number of private clubs, there are around a dozen clubs open to non-members.

Traditional Thai sports
Takroh is the Thai national sport for the average man. A lightweight rattan ball is moved around with the head, the knees, the elbows, the shoulders, and the feet — anything but the hands. People play everywhere: on playing fields, in the street, and — in the case of the experts — on television. It is not unlike basketball in terms of speed and general pattern of play.
Thai boxing is the genuine national sport, and is a serious business: huge bets are placed on bouts. Prior to the first round, the boxers perform strange little dances in the ring. They also chant exactly prescribed incantations. A loud band plays folk

Thai boxing

melodies. When the boxers have done enough praying for victory and for their trainers, the merciless fighting can begin. It immediately becomes clear why Thai boxing is unique in the world: here they dish out punishment not only with their fists, but also by kicking their opponents. Elbows and knees can also be used. Fights take place on Thursdays and Sundays in Bangkok's Rajdamnern Stadium, and on Tuesdays and Saturdays in the Lumpini Arena, also in Bangkok.

Sword-fighting: this is an ancient Siamese fighting game involving dangerous-looking swords, often one in each hand. These fights are for display only, mainly for tourists. A variant uses thick bamboo poles. The sparks may not exactly fly, but when a sword or a bamboo pole splinters, the bits can fly out into the audience.

Kite fights are a popular fun sport. There are male kites, called *Chula*, and female, called *Pakpao*. With his jagged edges, the bigger, star-shape male tries to cut the end off the female's tail. The smaller female, by contrast, manoeuvres so as to try and wrap herself around the enemy's tail and drag him to the ground.

Animal fights are widespread, particularly in southern Thailand, with large audiences, and heavy betting. The biggest attraction is the Siamese *bullfight*. There is no matador, as bull is pitted against bull. More widespread is *cock-fighting*: Thai fighting cocks have particularly strong spurs, and thus fight without artificial ones. Most popular of all, however, are *fish-fighting* tournaments. The fish are specially bred, and are strong, wild, and marvellously beautiful. It is always two males which are placed in the tank, always two spectacularly colourful specimens. The fight generally lasts until the weaker fish has been bitten to death.

Fishing is not seen as a sport in Thailand, but as a kind of harvesting. People fish in every waterway, throughout the country. The *klongs* – the canals – in particular are teeming with fish.

Food and drink

If you are adventurous by nature you will eat fantastically in Thailand: exotic food comes in wholly unsuspected combinations, and it is almost always hot and spicy! If you were looking for a symbol to hang over any Thai kitchen, it would have to be a chilli. Thai cuisine makes abundant use of its fiery qualities.

In Bangkok you will find a never-ending supply of very good restaurants – Thai, Chinese, Indonesian, Japanese, Korean, and even European. The delights of Thai cuisine are not confined to high-class establishments. Even the food stalls on street corners or the vendors on narrow boats on the klongs offer first-class food, at ridiculously low prices. If you want to eat at one of these open-air stalls but cannot speak Thai – don't worry! You can always point, and smile.

The roots of Thai cuisine lie unmistakably in India and China. However, in contrast to the mainly mild nature of Chinese dishes, Thai cuisine is, as has been noted, hot and spicy. Hungarian and Serbian food is bland in comparison! But unlike Indian cuisine, whose favourite dishes are often too hot for the Westerner to taste properly, Thai dishes are prepared in such a way that the true flavour of the food is never 'lost' behind the hot spices.

Thai food needs to be spicy. It is heavy, and uses a great deal of pork dripping. The sweet foods are very sweet, the sour very sour. Thai chefs make great use of cardamom, basil, mint, lemon grass, and masses of coriander and garlic. And then they add the really hot spices, from the relatively mild *prikh chee fa* pepper to the chilli variety known as *prikh kee nu lueng*, which should not be handled without a firearms certificate!

Then there are the spices whose names are not familiar to us, and a whole arsenal of pastes and sauces whose subtlety allows comparison with the finest French culinary offerings – sauces made from unpeeled shrimps, from fish, fruit, vegetables and herbs. The Thais share the Indians' love of curry dishes. These are made of chicken, other meats, coconut milk, capers, vegetables and garlic. You can tell the waiter how hot you want them, or you can make your own adjustments by sprinkling your food with some of the powdered 'dynamite' served in tiny bowls alongside your curry. You eat with fork and spoon – the spoon in your right hand, the fork in your left. Chopsticks are found only in Chinese restaurants. There are no knives on the table, so all the food is cut into bite-sized pieces in the kitchen.

Except in a few specialist rice dishes, rice comes to the table either fried or plain 'white' (dry) – boiled with neither spice nor oils, and with just a little salt. The Thais share the Chinese passion for pork, but beef plays a minor role. Skilfully prepared and spiced, chicken dishes are particularly tasty, served in their spoon-sized morsels. Coconut milk is used for cooking, not cow's milk.

Like their Chinese cousins, the Thais are great lovers of soup. The average Thai meal consists almost always of a bowl of rice surrounded by half a dozen smaller bowls containing vegetables, fish, the inevitable soup, curry, and sauces made from ginger, plums, or shrimps – and of course chilli. The soup is served alongside the rice and the rest of the dishes, and all the courses are eaten simultaneously: a bit of chicken, a spoonful of soup, some rice, a few shrimps, more rice, the soup again, then more chicken, and the fish. Only the dessert is served separately, at the end of the meal. Cheese is never offered; the Thai digestive system is simply not prepared for it. Most Thais eat between 7 and 8 am, between noon and 1 pm, and around 6 pm.

Typical Thai dishes

During your first few days you would perhaps do well to trust in the more moderate style of hotel cuisine, which has been adjusted to suit the Western digestive system. The spices are toned down, and the range of food is more suited to tourist tastes. But once you are capable of dealing with a slightly larger amount of shredded chilli, you should allow yourself to enter the paradise of authentic Thai cuisine.

Although you are unlikely to have problems with drinking-water at your hotel, it is probably safer as a general rule to avoid it – you can always drink Thai whisky instead! You can of course drink mineral water (as long as it is in the original bottle with the seal unbroken). Wine has only been produced in Thailand over the last few years; it is sweet and heavy. Imported wines are expensive. Thai beer is first class, having won prizes in international competitions.

Gaeng chud gai

For 4–6 persons:
1 chicken, a bunch of herbs, 3 cloves of garlic, ground coriander, 250 g of fresh mushrooms, cane sugar, soy sauce, vinegar.

Wash the chicken and cook with the herbs and a teaspoon of salt in 2 litres of water for 45 minutes. Remove the bones and cut the meat into strips. Strain the juices and reduce a little. Wash the mushrooms and cut into quarters or eighths. Heat 3 tablespoons of vegetable oil in a pan and brown the crushed garlic cloves, stirring in 1 tablespoon of ground coriander and 1 teaspoon of white pepper. Add the strips of chicken and sprinkle with 1 tablespoon of sugar. Turn the chicken and allow to brown for a few minutes. As soon as the sugar starts to become caramelised, pour 1 ladleful of chicken stock over the mixture.

Put the contents of the pan and the fresh mushrooms into the chicken stock, bring to the boil for 3 minutes, and add 1 tablespoon of soy sauce and about 1 teaspoon of vinegar to taste.

Exotic fruit on display

Typical dishes

Naem song kroeng: pork sausage containing ginger and chilli.
Yam sapparod: pineapple with pork, shrimps and coconut.
Gai ob sapparod: chicken with pineapple, served in hollowed-out pineapple.
Hoy mang poo ob mor din: spicy mussels.
Satay gai: chicken cooked with peanut sauce.
Goong shoob pang tod: fried shrimps with a sweet, spicy sauce.
Loog shin goong pad pak sopon: little shrimp dumplings with vegetables.
Hoo chalarm pad hang: fried shark-fin with beansprouts.
Pad ped gob: fried frog in a very hot sauce.
Moo tod gratiam prik tai: fried pork with garlic and pepper sauce.
Gang keow warn nua: beef curry with coconut milk.
Nua pad king: pieces of fried beef with ginger.
Nong gai ob: leg of chicken in an oyster sauce.
Gai gra bueng: chicken and shrimp-meat in 'pancakes' with vegetables.
Ped toon: duck soup with durum wheat noodles.

Barbecued bananas for sale

Tom yam goong: crayfish soup with lemon and chilli.
Gang chud hoy nang rom: oyster soup.
Gang tai pla: spicy vegetable soup with salted fish.
Kao pad gaeno gai: fried rice with chicken curry.
Kao clook gapi: fried rice with shrimp paste and sweet pork.
Salim: noodles with coconut milk, served ice cold.
Tab tim grob: water chestnuts in coconut milk.
Kai jeow moosub: a sort of omelette with crayfish meat.
Pla too: fried salted mackerel.
Mee krob: sweet crispy noodles, shrimps, and shredded plantain.

Silver souvenirs in the making

Shopping – the great temptation

Even those tourists who start off with no intention of souvenir-hunting tend to get drawn into it in Thailand. The first thing you think of, quite naturally, is Thai silk. It has changed a lot in recent years, from the rather coarse-napped and mainly single-coloured product to a much lighter one, often patterned and in more subdued shades. Heavy-quality silks are more expensive than the lightweight ones. If you are offered something unusually cheap, make sure you are not looking at artificial silk or polyester!

You are pretty certain to find high-quality products in the better shops. The TAT (Tourism Authority of Thailand) produces a little free brochure listing reliable shops – the *Thailand Shopping Guide*.

What makes Thailand and particularly Bangkok so seductive is the low prices demanded for top-quality goods. This applies to silk, but also to cotton goods, silverware, leather, antiques, bronze and jewellery. If you are so inclined you can no doubt push the price down further by haggling.

Gold, silver and certain gemstones are all sold very cheaply in Thailand. The best value is in gemstones, above all sapphires but also Burmese rubies. Since tourists can seldom assess the quality of a stone, and gifted Thai forgers are always busy at their trade, you will find yourself exposed to exorbitant prices and to the risk of buying imitation stones if you stray beyond the shops of good repute.

The same goes for antiques. In Bangkok you can wander past hundreds of antique-shops, amazed and astonished at where this vast horde of antiques comes from. Serious dealers make no secret of it: many pieces – statues, temple ornaments, furniture – are imitations, although they may well be carved from ancient wood. Dealers will always assure you that they can easily obtain the necessary export permit for you from the *Fine Arts Department*, as well as all the papers for shipping your purchases home. The same rule applies here: you can trust the officially recommended shops. In a few months' time your carvings will indeed arrive

Shopping – the great temptation

at your home address. But beware of Buddhas! The exporting of Buddha figures has been banned for some years now, whether they are real antiques, imitations, or brand new. In the Chiang Mai region there are entire factories producing reliefs and carved figures – tigers, elephants, horses, buffaloes, saints and dancers – as well as exquisite mirror frames. It is worth paying a visit here, since the rates are very favourable. And somewhere among the quantities of goods you can always find first-class pieces made in the ancient Siamese tradition: painted, gilded, plain or spangled, and all carved from top-quality teak.

Of the greatest interest are the ancient Chinese porcelains, Thai porcelains and stoneware, Burmese temple carvings covered in gold leaf, watches, and paintings.

One branch of the souvenir industry has in recent years specialised in copies and imitations, or, to be more precise, forgeries. The objects made are sold as forgeries, the best-known being copies of really expensive Swiss or French watches. Many shops sell them on a discreet basis – in a back room and only if the customer specifically asks for one. But Bangkok's street traders have no such qualms, offering entire collections of top-brand European watches, all fakes. It is not only watches that are faked: luxury leather-goods from France and Italy, pens and brand-name textiles all suffer the same treatment. If you should be tempted to buy one of the dirt-cheap fake watches just for a joke, remember that the importing of illegal copies is a punishable offence in many countries.

Prices for made-to-measure clothing are another huge temptation, whether you buy trousers, jackets, suits, blouses, shirts, evening wear, dinner jackets or safari suits. Many tailors offer to have your goods ready within twenty-four hours, including a fitting session. More reliable are those who offer two fittings and take three days. The materials are all of exemplary quality, but you should pay close attention during your fittings because the workmanship is sometimes rather slipshod. It is also advisable to take with you a fashion magazine or a piece of clothing from which the unseen, mainly Indian, tailors can work – unless you are capable of giving precise and unmistakable orders regarding style and cut.

In the major department stores and the luxury shops prices are fixed, with no reductions. But in every other kind of shop haggling is permissible. The shopkeepers expect it and right from the outset offer quite good reductions, which can be made even better depending on the skill of the customer. You are not advised to use any of the 'touts' whose job it is to steer the foreigner to particular jewellers, tailors, and restaurants. The commission paid to the tout is always added on to the customer's bill.

If you buy cutlery made of gold-coloured bronze, be sure that it has a protective layer of silicon. Without it, the inevitable stains will be very hard to get rid of.

Shopping centres – the new temples

You are very likely to be enticed into one of the city's new shopping centres, if only because here you can escape the merciless heat outside and enjoy the air-conditioned coolness. You will find yourself in the *Siam Center*, perhaps, right next to the Siam International Hotel. Or in *Rajadamri Arcade*, or *Pratunam*. And there are a dozen others, alongside the Royal Orchard Sheraton and in Ploenchit Road, and all over this huge metropolis. All of them are bursting with antiques, made-to-measure tailoring, silk, leather, jewellery, dolls and ceramics of the finest quality.

Wai and wat

Unlike Western customs, etiquette in Thailand is an intricate, inexorable, but gentle and gracious system of gestures, signs, and even omissions. These always have a deeper meaning, and frequently a social background stretching back hundreds of years.

As soon as you arrive at the airport, Thailand's omnipresent way of greeting and showing respect, the *wai*, becomes evident. It looks at first sight quite straightforward. The hands are pressed together and moved towards the head. But the wai is more than a simple customary greeting. It is offered in hundreds of gradations: quick and almost casual, pious with a slight or deep bow, with the hands pressed together in front of the chest, or near the neck, or over the forehead. All these versions of the wai mean something quite different. If two people of equal rank or two strangers greet each other, for instance, the thumbs touch the chest, but the fingertips do not quite reach the chin.

But now the subtleties begin. You greet somebody of higher rank by making your fingertips touch your nose. A person of lower rank has to be content when the fingertips of his boss, or some rich man, or an important customer, or any person to be respected, fall far short of the nose. If, though, you are trying to signal the utmost admiration, reverence, or subordination, the thumbs are raised as high as the forehead, and the upper body bows quite distinctly. This is also the traditional method of showing respect towards a monk, a shrine, sacred objects, or gods. The Thai people will even greet monuments, shrines and trees in this manner from a moving bus.

And what will you do? Well, you will probably soon feel tempted to respond to the charming habit of the wai. If you mean it seriously, and if you do not offend too obviously against the strict regulations, then the Thai will be only too pleased to see a friendly foreigner using the wai. But anyone mimicking it just for fun is doing himself and the Thai people no favour at all.

Grand Palace, Bangkok

Temple of the Emerald Buddha (Wat Phra Keo), Bangkok

The whole thing is even more complicated than it seems: if the social distance between two Thais is very great, the higher-placed one does not even return the greeting. The beggar's wai receives no response, and neither are children and servants honoured with the wai.

You might perhaps find these social gradations out of date, undemocratic, and even immoral. But if you react by answering the street-sweeper, or some little shrimp of a beggar, or your chambermaid, with a grand wai, you will cause them dreadful embarrassment, and any Thai standing in the vicinity will probably laugh out loud at you.

Of course, the wai has a real historical pedigree. It indicates that the hands raised to the head are carrying no weapons. You will soon notice that the wai is used not only for greeting but also to express thanks. In the latter case, you must not respond to it: a smile will do.

Wai and *wat* – two indispensable concepts in Thailand. The *wat* is just the name for a temple. The shimmering gold and the atmosphere of the incense-filled temples make them one of the great sights of Thailand.

Other customs: a brief etiquette

Thailand is a polite country. The stranger is treated with respect. People smile, and the best thing is to smile back. A foreigner might get annoyed if a taxi-driver cannot find the address he has been given, or if the traces of tailor's chalk have not been removed from a made-to-measure jacket. But there is one thing he must not do: allow his displeasure to show in his voice, or his gestures, or in an angry glance. To do so would be to lose face. In Thailand you always stay cool. Emotions are not displayed. You smile.

Some other rules should be observed at all cost. Regardless of whether a particular *wat* is a building of the highest artistic quality or a simple barn in a rice-growers' village, it demands respect from the foreigner. You may only enter barefoot and bareheaded. Do not step on the threshold in any doorway: this is deemed unseemly and damaging. Visitors may not enter a particularly strict wat if they are wearing short-sleeved shirts, or, in the case of women, clothing that is too light and airy, or shorts, or mini-skirts. Women are not allowed to give anything directly to monks, and they may not speak to them; under no circumstances may a woman touch a monk. Disrespectful behaviour, joke photographs and loud laughter in a wat are even punishable by law. You should never touch a Thai on the head, and never show the soles of your feet or of your shoes. Avoid crossing your legs, since it could be interpreted as pointing towards someone with your foot, which is not done.

You will immediately notice how scrupulously clean and tidy the Thais keep their clothing. Nowhere in the entire country will you come across anyone dressed in rags. The Thais take frequent baths, and dirt and dust are immediately swept up or washed away.

And what about the beach? Going naked is absolutely taboo. Going topless is not tolerated around swimming pools, or on the beaches used mainly by Thais. In the small bays belonging to the tourist hotels it has become common, despite the fact that it is severely violating the official codes of decency.

Strict rules apply when visiting the Grand Palace in Bangkok. Men are obliged to wear trousers, jackets and ties, women dresses or trousers and shoes. Just in case you should meet the King, you will be highly relieved to hear that you are no longer forced to do what was obligatory on pain of death in earlier times: crawl towards His Majesty on all fours.

Things you do not mention

Thailand is not without its contradictions. On the one hand, you can find absolutely every form of nightlife. In the 'massage parlours' of Bangkok and Chiang Mai – from simple houses to luxury palaces decorated with dazzling gold and marble – nobody would expect the kind of treatment offered by a medical practitioner for health reasons. Massage parlours have become so successfully established that they almost constitute an industry in themselves. The development of the red-light districts in the capital – Patpong and Sukhumvit Road, with its many alleyways to either side – has been encouraged not least by the 'farang' (a distortion of 'foreigner').

On the other hand, Thailand is deemed very demure. The all-pervading figure of Buddha condemns carnal lust, and even a husband and wife holding hands in public are seen as improper. There is no nakedness on television or in the cinema, let alone bedroom scenes. Foreign males should always treat Thai women with respect.

Hints for your holiday

Thailand is the perfect place to take a holiday if you like things hot and exotic, but at the same time highly civilised. This country, lying between the foothills of the Himalayas and the Gulf of Thailand, has everything one could ask of a modern paradise: jungle, beaches as white as snow, an advanced civilisation, exotic cuisine, elephants and tigers, a generally first-class road system and air links, flawless service, and people whose warmth continually overwhelms the visitor. And since the low prices are also an amazing feature, one tends to bring a whole sackful of souvenirs back from Thailand: gold and gemstones, made-to-measure clothes, leather goods, silks in all the colours of the tropical rainbow, antiques, spices, bowls, candlesticks and rings. One thing you cannot bring back is a Buddha. The export of Buddhas is forbidden not because there is any shortage of them – there are probably more representations of Buddha than there are people in Thailand. No, the reason is to prevent Buddha from becoming a cheap curio for souvenir-hunters. After all, the smiling Buddha forms the religious core of the nation, and is revered in many thousands of temples from the impenetrable mountain forests of the north to the Malayan isthmus deep in the equatorial south.

What a country! Orchids, skyscrapers, the Bridge over the River Kwai, curry, spirit houses, water buffaloes, windsurfing, rice, rice, and more rice, electronics, poppyfields, and tuk-tuks, the motor-bike taxis. It is inexhaustible.... Don't forget the word for pleasure, delight, fun, and feeling good: it is *sanuk*.

View over Menam River, Bangkok

Where to go and what to see

Bangkok Pop. 6 million approx.

The capital city, Bangkok, is not actually called Bangkok at all. Its real name (abbreviated) is *Krung Thep*, or City of Angels. And the Menam River on which it lies is not called the Menam but *Mae Nam Chao Phraya*, or Mother of All Waters. Thirty-three kilometres before it discharges into the Gulf of Thailand, the mighty river describes an almost semicircular curve. This is where the victorious Thai General Taksin wanted his kingdom's capital relocated in 1767, and that is precisely what happened. The site was called *Thonburi*, and lay on the right bank. Fifteen years later, the capital was relocated once again, this time to the left bank, to Bang Kok. Since those days, the insatiable giant Bangkok has completely swallowed up its little twin.

When Bangkok was still brand new, it had no streets at all, only its canals, or *klongs*. Nowadays it is one big continuous traffic jam. The sultry heat presses down on to the exhaust gases; after a few minutes, freshly laundered shirt-collars are turned dark brown. Bangkok is a loud place. The smells also shout out at you. There are miles and miles of wretched boredom: its drab grey slums. The people either sit still or run. Crossing any main road, they scuttle for dear life. Drivers in Bangkok like to keep the accelerator flat down. They don't smile.

This place plays strange tricks with your sense of direction. There is a strict system of one-way streets, and then there are streets which do not even appear on the city map — and no amount of silent cursing will improve the situation. The city is vast. It seems impossible to take a taxi ride lasting less than half an hour. An explosive building-boom has studded the chaos of little houses with white skyscrapers and has criss-crossed it with eight-lane avenues.

Impressions

Crowded around the feet of Bangkok's glass and concrete towers are its retail shopping areas: dilapidated little shops amongst the geometry of functional towers. There are sterile green areas, of the sort laid out by municipal gardeners in Europe around the turn of the century. There are blind beggars, and legless beggars.

A procession passes by. Musicians up front. Happy parents, happy friends, a happy young monk just accepted into the order. Bird cages with tiny little birds hopping around inside them; you can buy their freedom. Suddenly a hot, spicy smell lashes the senses: a stand selling dried fish. The chatter of a machine gun: false alarm, it is only a tuk-tuk, one of Bangkok's 10,000 three-wheeler motorbike taxis. Suddenly, above the low rooftops, a golden spire. As you approach, it turns into a white mountain: *Phu Khao Thong*, the Golden Mount. An artificial white hill with paths winding their way round it. On top, a golden plateau, and above this a golden cone, like the most beautiful top to a Christmas tree. Phu Khao Thong is like an Everest in the middle of this tropical ants' nest. A place of flawless beauty, a kind of Acropolis. Of course, it is a temple. It guards a relic of Buddha. You arrive at the top, bathed in sweat. You see a panorama over the City of Angels – and all at once the steaming, blaring metropolis is made to seem nothing by a forest of golden towers.

The attraction of Bangkok lies in its contradictions and contrasts. The best sights are almost exclusively temples. What lies between them seems almost to have been casually scattered: masses of little shops, flats, canals, street kitchens, workshops, warehouses, ministries, streets crowded to bursting-point, pedestrian footbridges, tower-block hotels, shacks, vegetable-stalls, junk-dealers, luxury shops, fortune-tellers, lorries full of freshly made Buddhas, the reinforced-concrete skeletons of houses. The city sprawls on and on.

Tuk-tuks

You will find them in Chiang Mai and in Pattaya, but the bulk of them are found of course in the capital: the ubiquitous tuk-tuks. They are actually called *sam-lor*, but the nickname of tuk-tuk reproduces in any language the kind of noise they make. Tuk-tuks are gaudy, with a fringed awning, and look like a cross between an open rickshaw and a motorbike: behind the front section there is a two-man seat mounted above the two rear wheels. They would never pass a roadworthiness test for passenger-carrying vehicles – but neither would the narrow passenger-boats plying the klongs! In recent years, the tuk-tuk has become an ever-present, cheap form of taxi. In the evening, when the tuk-tuks are all lit up with rows of coloured lightbulbs, you feel you are getting into something resembling a cheap nightclub. The roaring traffic with its exhaust fumes seems only centimetres away. There is a strict rule for riding in tuk-tuks: always agree the fare in advance. You will pay the farangs' (foreigners') fare anyway – much dearer than the fare for Thais, but still reasonable.

Bangkok

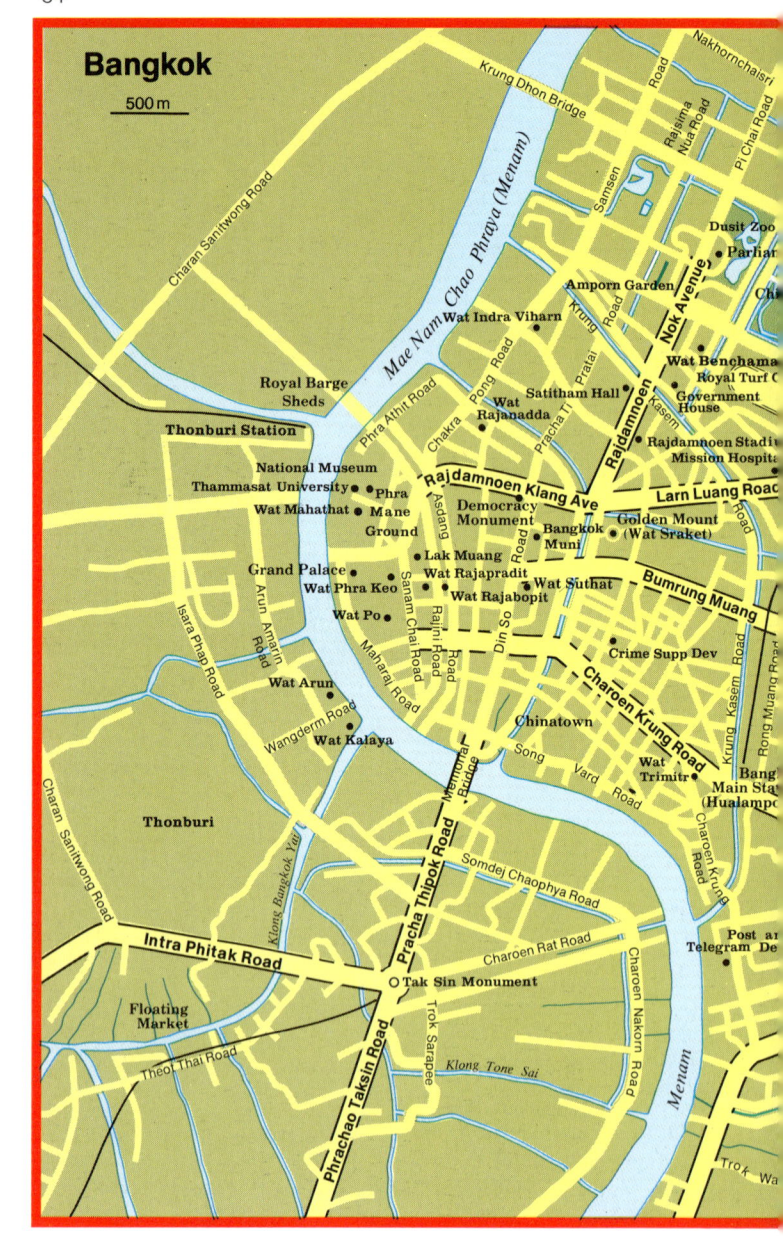

500 m

- Krung Dhon Bridge
- Nakhornchaisri Road
- Rajsima Nua Road
- Pt. Chai Road
- Charan Sanitwong Road
- Samsen Road
- Mae Nam Chao Phraya (Menam)
- Dusit Zoo
- Parliar
- Amporn Garden
- Wat Indra Viharn
- Krung Road
- Nok Avenue
- Cha
- Pong Road
- Pra Chai
- Wat Benchama
- Royal Turf C
- Royal Barge Sheds
- Phra Athit Road
- Satitham Hall
- Kasem
- Government House
- Thonburi Station
- Chakra Road
- Wat Rajanadda
- Rajdamnoen
- Rajdamnoen Stadi
- Mission Hospit:
- National Museum
- Thammasat University
- Phra
- Asdang Road
- Rajdamnoen Klang Ave
- Wat Mahathat
- Mane Ground
- Democracy Monument
- Bangkok Muni
- Golden Mount (Wat Sraket)
- Larn Luang Road
- Grand Palace
- Wat Phra Keo
- Wat Rajapradit
- Lak Muang
- Wat Suthat
- Wat Po
- Wat Rajabopit
- Bumrung Muang
- Arun Amarin Road
- Sanam Chai Road
- Rajni Road
- Din So Road
- Isara Phap Road
- Maharaj Road
- Crime Supp Dev
- Charoen Krung Road
- Krung Kasem Road
- Rong Muang Road
- Wat Arun
- Wanggerm Road
- Chinatown
- Wat Kalaya
- Song Vard Road
- Wat Trimitr
- Bang Main Sta (Hualompo
- Thonburi
- Klong Bangkok Yai
- Memorial Bridge
- Somdej Chaophya Road
- Charoen Krung Road
- Charan Sanitwong Road
- Pracha Thipok Road
- Charoen Rat Road
- Post ar Telegram De
- Intra Phitak Road
- Tak Sin Monument
- Charoen Nakorn Road
- Floating Market
- Theot Thai Road
- Phrachao Taksin Road
- Trok Sarapee
- Klong Tone Sai
- Menam
- Tro Wa

35

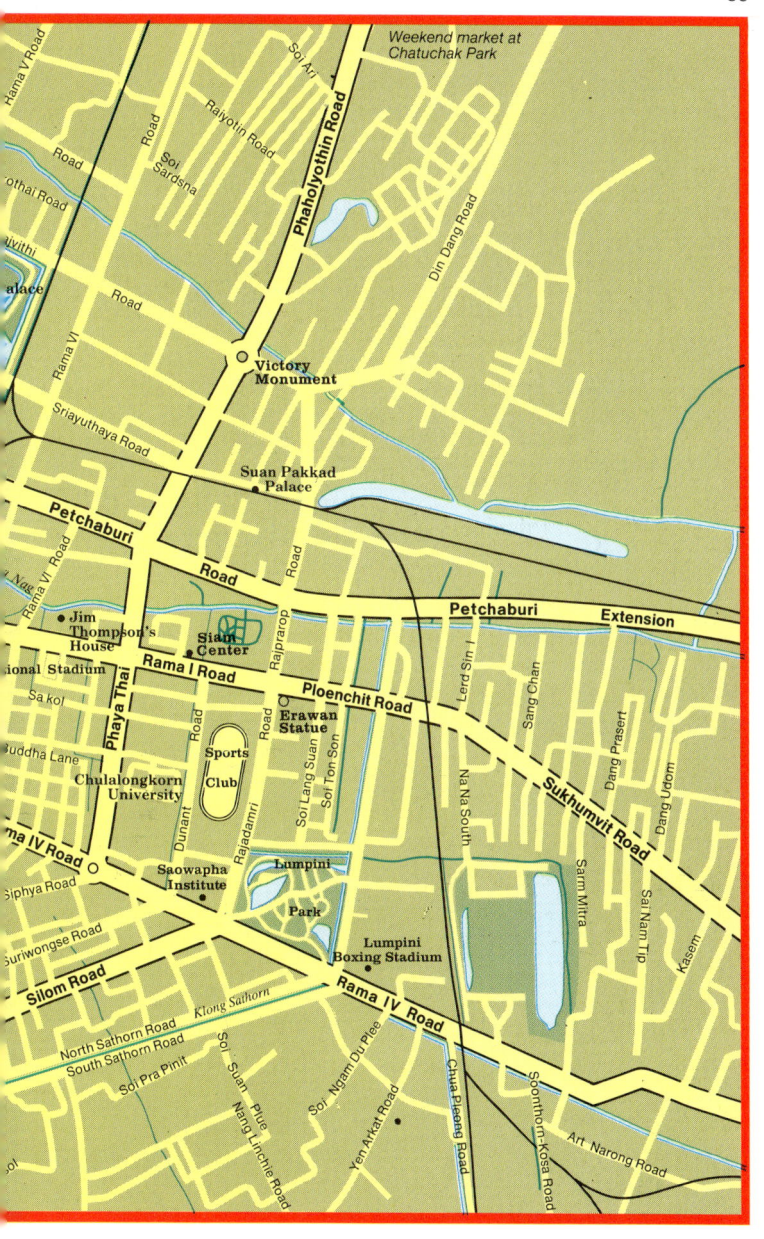

Wat Phra Keo and Grand Palace, Bangkok

📷 A trip round Bangkok

Before visiting the sights you should simply wander round a bit. First get your hotel porter to give you a little card with the hotel's name and address written on it in Thai, so that you can indicate to a taxi-driver who doesn't speak English exactly where you want to be dropped off. The porter will also tell you what price to pay for the taxi. The best hotels for foreigners share a limousine service. In the foyer, there is a transport organiser who writes down on a slip of paper where you want to go. You pay straight away, and not in the taxi. With this system, tips are not necessary. Outside, a second man will pull up in a fully air-conditioned taxi just for you. This limousine service is of course more expensive than normal taxis. And you would be wasting your time to try to haggle over the fare. You only get the best service, and you are never cheated.

Ordinary taxis can be hailed from the kerb. At this point you should agree the fare, or even haggle, for as yet there are no meters in Bangkok's taxis!

Your first stroll around will bombard you with a welter of impressions: the roar of the city, its smells, its working life, what the people eat, and even how the city conceals its true face. If you want to uncover the delights of Bangkok in a systematic manner – as you should – you can book a sightseeing tour; otherwise just make a list of all the things you want to see.

The area round the royal palace

Bangkok's official name is so long and so pompous that hardly anybody can say it without prompting. Translated, it means City of Angels; Great City; Residence of the Emerald Buddha; Invincible City of the Goddess Indra; Great Capital of the World, furnished with the Nine Precious Gemstones; Fortunate City of Great Regal Palaces resembling the Celestial Home where God Incarnate resides; City given by Indra and built by Vishnu Karman. This resounding name applies to the area around the royal palace, with the palace itself and the two great neighbouring monastery complexes of Wat Phra Keo and Wat Po. If you have not visited these two great sites, you have not seen Bangkok. This is probably the best place to start your systematic exploration of Bangkok – where the city's long history began.

The royal palace (Grand Palace, or Chakri Maha Phrasad) formed the core of modern Thailand under the Chakri dynasty. King Rama I started its construction in 1782. Providing they are decently dressed, visitors are allowed to enter some of the innumerable, vastly elaborate and endlessly interconnecting rooms in the palace. These rooms are not for living in, but merely for show. (Opening times: 8.30–11.30 am, 1–3.30 pm daily.)

The white, gold and pale yellow colouring is splendidly impressive. Then you suddenly stop and stare in amazement: you seem to be looking at a Renaissance palace topped with golden pagoda-like towers. But this is easily explained: it was an Englishman who built the bulk of the residence in 1882, but the decoration was entrusted to local experts. Visitors are bound to notice the unusually extravagant roofs, both here and on other major buildings in Thailand: above an elongated roof there sits a shorter one, and above that a shorter one still. This triple structure is not merely intended to signal great wealth, but has a practical purpose: air can circulate between the various roof levels and be cooled down a degree or two.

The inner chambers of the former harem are still closed to the public. The present King and his beautiful Queen do not live in the Grand Palace, but in *Chitralada Palace*, outside the old palace quarter. This might perhaps have something to do with the dreadful events of 1946, when the young King Ananda was found shot dead in his bed. The murder of the young King has not been solved to this day. He was succeeded by his younger brother, Bhumibol Adulyadej, who was crowned in 1947.

Wat Phra Keo

Next you reach the area of the Temple of the Emerald Buddha, or Wat Phra Keo. This is Bangkok's temple of temples. It is not particularly old, but then nothing in the capital is really old. King Rama I had the building started in 1785, and although at the time no contacts existed with leading European designers, what emerged was a kind of Indo-Chinese Rococo style. Glitteringly colourful façades and mirrored mosaics shimmer in the intense tropical sunlight, demons bare their teeth, dragons and grotesque giants stand guard – and they

The royal palace

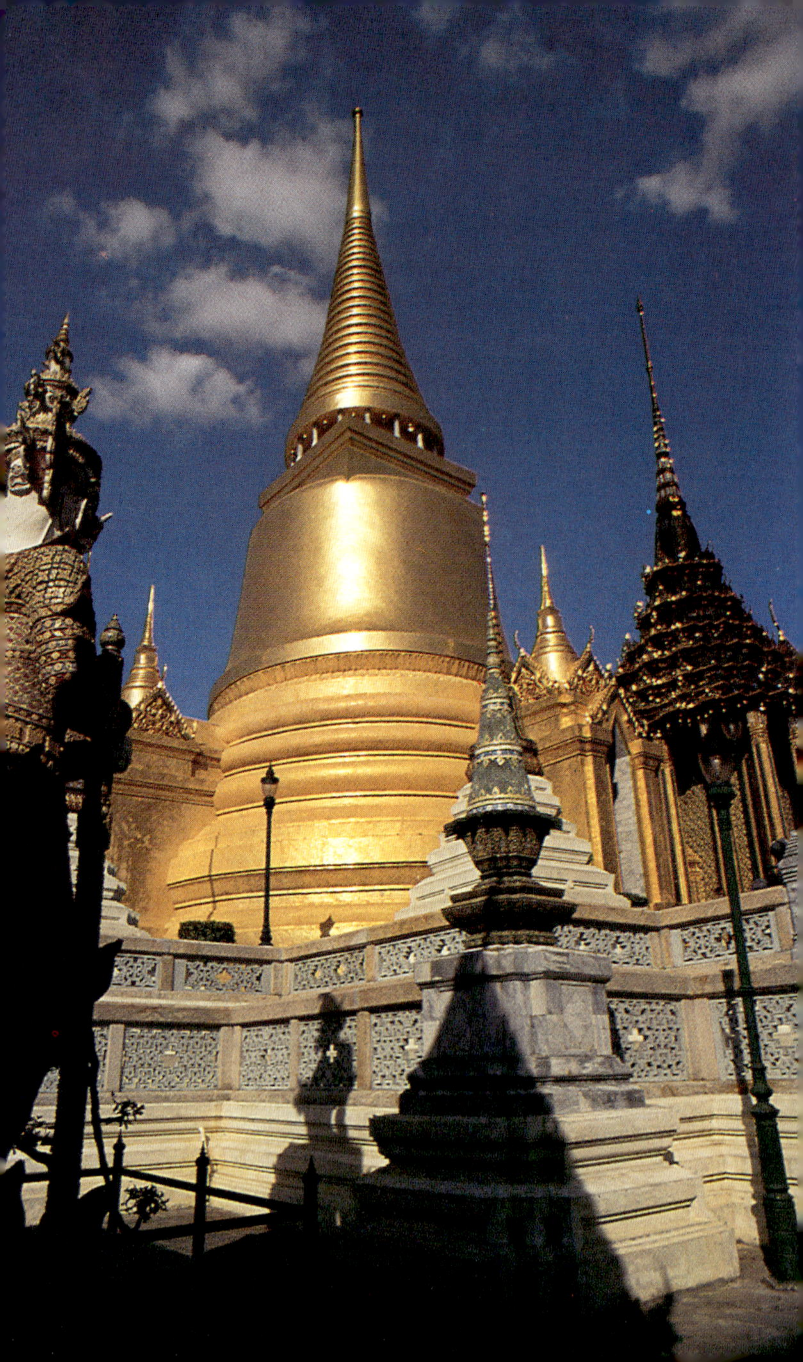

all look a little like clowns. Everything is so pompously stylised that even the most ferocious lions look more like sweet little pedigree poodles. Photographs just cannot reproduce the scale of the towers, all the nooks and crannies, the stairways and balustrades, nor of course the merciless heat, the sweet trails of scent left by the incense sticks, the cries of the exotic birds, the aura of garlic, the coolness of the stone floor under one's feet.

The King himself prays here to the Emerald Buddha, clothing it afresh for each of the three seasons in the Thai year, as only the King may do. Where is the throne of the Emerald Buddha? In the gloom of the holy of holies. Warm winds blow through the open slit windows, disturbing the temple's thousands of little brass bells. Every inch of the inside of the Temple of the Emerald Buddha is painted: the life-story of Buddha depicted in vivid chapters for those of the faithful who cannot read. The Emerald Buddha is suspended high up in an electronically protected glass case. He is no bigger than a new-born child. The jewel-encrusted gold robe which the King puts on him almost completely envelops the figure of the Buddha.

Far below, the offerings left by the wealthy lie piled up: a heap of items dripping with gold. To all Buddhists the Emerald Buddha counts as a sacred and venerable shrine of the first magnitude. The figure of Buddha, a mere 75 cm high, used to stand in the northern Thai city of Chiang Rai in the 15th c. It found its way to Thonburi in 1778 and to Bangkok in 1784, having previously travelled via Lampang, Chiang Mai, Luang Prabang, and Vientiane, in Laos.

In 1987, for the sixtieth birthday of King Bhumibol, the entire temple area

Above: Temple guard, Wat Phra Keo
Below: Inside the temple complex

Left: Wat Phra Keo

was thoroughly renovated. The gold now glistens, the colours dazzle, and the demons grimace in a display of renewed youthful vigour. The Thais' attitude to preserving monuments differs sharply from the aims of European conservationists, who try to avoid covering up the real antiquity of an endangered building when renovating it. No, the attitude is quite different here, and Wat Phra Keo now looks brand new. If you can only manage to see one temple, make it this one!

Formal elements typical of all Thai monasteries (*wats*) may be distinguished in the Emerald Buddha Temple complex. First, there is the central shrine, or *bot*, where the monks conduct their ceremonies; alongside this lies the second important room, the *vihara*, which is intended more as a place where all the faithful may pray, and which is not quite as splendid. *Chedi* are the cone-shaped structures where holy relics are housed; their origins are to be found in India and Ceylon. The whole structure stands on a number of layers of concealed brickwork made into a stepped wall which tapers off towards the top.

The *prang* is equally unmistakable. A narrow, straight tower, usually highly decorated, it derives from Khmer origins in what is now Kampuchea. The prang has four niches in its base. One of these houses the reliquary, which can only be reached via a steep and narrow flight of stone steps. The ornamental part of the tower rises just above the reliquary. Thailand's most famous prang stands within the splendid Wat Arun, on the other bank of the river, one of Bangkok's unmistakable landmarks. Other significant features inside Wat Phra Keo are the so-called *Pantheon* – which has little in common with the ancient building of that name – containing statues of the kings of the Chakri dynasty; the *library*; a model of that wonder of the Asiatic world *Angkor Wat*; the *vihan yot*, an assembly hall splendidly decorated with coloured tiles; and the royal columbarium, *Phra Nak*, under its stepped roof.

Wat Po

The royal palace area adjoins the second great temple complex in Bangkok, Wat Po, which is officially known as *Wat Phra Chetubon* and virtually forms a holy city in itself: a labyrinth of opulent gold spires, courtyards, porticos, stairways, galleries and squares. If you join a sightseeing group, you will be whisked through in half an hour. Much better to come alone and stay for three hours. Wat Po is the Temple of the Reclining Buddha. Children have made the temple famous throughout the world by taking rubbings of its bas-reliefs on rice-paper. These highly decorative imprints now hang in living rooms all over the world. The great Temple of the Reclining Buddha is very much a building of and for the people. Within its strong walls there is a smell of cooking, as various stalls see to the needs of exhausted pilgrims. Hens cackle. Monks pad silently across the courtyards. Tatters of paper streamers provide reminders of bygone festivals. To ward off barrenness, childless women decorate a huge male member made of stone.

Wat Po houses a gallery containing 394 Buddhas, as well as scientific and religious paintings, inscriptions, frescos, and high-quality Chinese stone figures which were allegedly brought here as ballast so that ships which were insufficiently laden could attain the correct depth in the water. The heavy teak doors to the temple are rightly counted as masterpieces of Siamese craftsmanship. King Rama I had major works of art

Inside Wat Po

Wat Po

brought to Wat Po from the ruins of the country's former great cities, and this explains the extravagant wealth of relics, statues and images, all of which must naturally be given a regal setting. Neither Rama I nor Rama III cut any corners: there are ninety chedis alone adorning the corners of Wat Po. And then there are the gardens, and the ceramic mosaics in gold and blue, and numerous courtyards, with yet more statues of Buddha. Then you are suddenly standing in front of the Great Reclining Buddha.

He is gigantic – bigger than Polyphemus in his cave! The *vihan phra non* hall of prayer was built around the Buddha, fitted to him like a robe. So there he lies all in gold, 49 m long and 12 m high, depicted at the moment of entry into Nirvana. The figure is made of brick covered in plaster, and is clothed in gold. Unfortunately, he is sick: traffic vibration, dense clouds of clinging exhaust, and the hothouse atmosphere in Bangkok have caused yard-long cracks to appear in the giant. Renovation work has been going on for years, and now he is lying quite comfortably again. The precious depictions on the soles of his huge feet are now quite clear to the eye.

Wat Arun

On the other bank of the Menam, in Bangkok's twin town of Thonburi, stands the third of the three great temples: the Temple of the Morning Twilight, or Wat Arun, where the rays of the morning sun light up the gilded figures, the glass inlays, and the porcelain decorations. In order to admire the cool austerity and the almost arrogantly erect isolation of the main tower at its best, it is advisable not to go to the monastery itself. It is enough to stand on the opposite bank:

Wat Arun

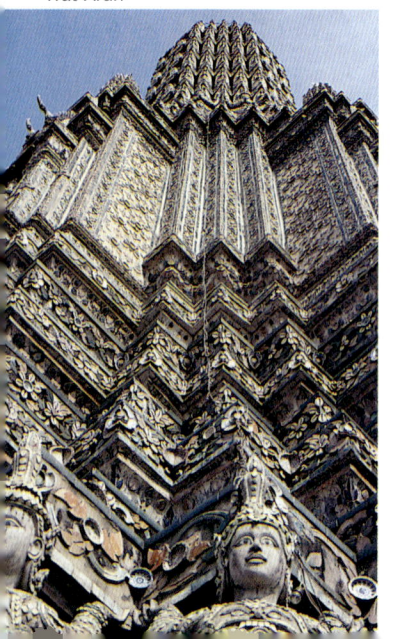

from this distance, and seen over the water, Wat Arun makes an unforgettable impression.

It is the oldest temple in Bangkok, and its structure is clearly of Khmer origin. Four moderately tall *prangs* confront you like servants or altar boys, and symbolise the four oceans of the world. They are merely the supporting cast for the entry of the *great prang*, an incomparably elegant pyramid 80 m high, with a refined structure and stepped sides of unusual design. From here, there is a beautiful view over the city. The temple may be reached by boat from the Hotel Oriental pier and from many stopping-points along the river. If you are not afraid of heights, try the steep flight of steps climbing up outside the prang. The view from the top is really worth the effort – over the broad, flowing Menam and the strange 'skin' of Wat Arun, made from pieces of coloured Chinese porcelain. When the porcelain ran out during the course of construction, King Rama III appealed to his subjects for help. The result was that from all over the kingdom cartloads of broken plates, dishes, teapots, ladles and bowls began to arrive.

Other temples

Golden Mount is in the grounds of *Wat Sraket* monastery. The only really high ground in Bangkok, it provides a view over the endless expanse of housing surrounding the city. It is built on the remains of a collapsed shrine, and its architecture is quite charming.

Wat Trimitr, with the Temple of the Golden Buddha; interesting history.

Wat Suthat, with its fine murals and Buddha images, and its Giant Swing.

Wat Benchama Bopitr is the marble temple. Well worth seeing for its famous collection of Buddha statues.

Bangkok

Museums and palaces
The National Museum has some of the very best Thai art. (Guided tours are available in English.)
Suan Pakkad Palace is a picture-book example of aristocratic domestic architecture, with gardens and pavilions.
Jim Thompson's Thai House comprises seven houses in splendid, ancient Thai style, lying in a beautiful park. They owe their preservation to the 'inventor' of Thai silk. Exquisite art collection.

Public buildings
The Democracy Monument has no real artistic merit, but is historically significant. Erected in 1933 to commemorate the declaration of a constitutional monarchy, it became the focus for student riots in June 1973, and in October 1973 witnessed the student revolt which led to the collapse of the government.

Wat Benchama Bopitr

The government buildings and other public buildings in Bangkok are of no interest: it is enough just to drive past them. The same is true for all the modern monuments: none is worth going out of your way for.

Markets
The *weekend market at Chatuchak Park* in Phaholyothin Road is open on Saturdays and Sundays from 7 am to 6 pm. You can wander here for hours on end among all manner of stalls. The displays of fruit and vegetables, local flowers and other kinds of plants are overwhelming. The city's other big markets will amaze you and make you reach for your camera: try *Bangrak*, *Klong*, *Toey* and *Pratunam*.

Chinatown
Almost a third of Bangkok's residents are Chinese or of Chinese descent. For a long time, all trade in the capital was dominated by the Chinese, and the major banking businesses are still in Chinese hands. The same is true of another vital branch of business: the gold trade. And it goes without saying that the Chinese element in this huge conurbation is most evident — being more visible, more audible, and more unmistakable to the nose and the palate — in Bangkok's Chinatown, or Sampeng.

Unlike the Chinatowns in New York or San Francisco, which exist within fairly strict confines, Bangkok's equivalent has no reliably definable boundaries. Chinatown starts just to the east of the Grand Palace, and wherever you get out of your taxi along the New Road (Charoen Krung) you will find yourself in the middle of it.

Should you be tempted to complain that in the rest of Bangkok Western influence has come too much to the fore – in the shape of too many palatial hotels, skyscrapers, embassies and shopping centres – you will not find the slightest trace of any of this in Chinatown. This is the true Orient: loud, seemingly even hotter and more chaotic, and even less penetrable. It is a real jungle of shops and markets, workshops, hostels and eating places. It smells of garlic and joss-sticks, and its hundreds of shop windows overflow with little gold chains and amulets, with porcelain, and with odd-looking implements whose function remains a complete mystery to the foreigner. Chinatown has its own clothes market; you are advised to be on your guard against pickpockets here.

If you only have an hour to spend in Chinatown, then start in *Sampeng Lane* (Soi Wanit), a pedestrian zone near Memorial Bridge. It has everything: letter-writers, paper lanterns, turquoise-blue stones, gold, and the limitless abundance of the tropical Far East – an adventure for the taste-buds and for the wallet.

The klongs – Bangkok's waterways

Bangkok's picturesque network of waterways was once so dense that it did not take long for people to make an obvious comparison and label the city 'the Venice of the Far East'. The city's subsoil is still so marshy that Bangkok continues to sink centimetre by centimetre. The bulk of the canals, or klongs, have been filled in because the space they occupied could be used more profitably as building-land or for roads. But the metropolis is still crossed by silent boats gliding past rows of open wooden houses, and what remains of the old system of navigable canals is still working as in former days. If you are visiting the house belonging to Jim Thompson, which has been world famous for many years, you will arrive via an absolutely typical klong: people live on *Klong Maha Nag*, it forms a watery highway and a swimming pool, is used by children as a playground, and makes a superb photograph.

One of the best sights in Bangkok lies on one of its perimeter klongs: the famous *Floating Market*, on Klong Dao Kanong. It is well worth visiting – unless you can afford the time to go to the more unspoilt, original floating market, on the Klong Damnoen Saduak, one and a half hours to the south-west, on the way to the Bridge over the River Kwai.

You can reach the Klong Dao Kanong market by speedboat: these slim, roaring vehicles serve as public transport. On the way, you will pass through some typical klongs and think you are travelling through some picture-book or other – women washing their clothes and themselves; laughing, naked children flopping from their stilt houses into the greyish-lilac waters of the river; peasant women rowing their wares to market, laden with their day's offering of vegetables, fruit and spices; unfamiliar birds shrieking; orchids showing off their splendour; monkeys howling.

The morning traffic is so dense at the Floating Market that you can scarcely see the water. There isn't a single shop in Europe that could match the variety of vegetables on offer, in every shade of green, yellow and red. Many of the boats are tiny floating kitchens. The cook assembles her ingredients with the skill of a virtuoso: she grates and flash-fries some white vegetable, adds green herbs, flavours the mixture with a shot of some fiery red sauce, places in it some fish in breadcrumbs, and adds boiling broth straight from her charcoal stove, before putting in some pieces of chocolate-coloured meat, black mushrooms, and a final sprinkling of spices. The steaming bowl is immediately

The Floating Market in Bangkok

handed over to the next boat, where her neighbour begins to spoon the mixture out — pausing only to sell a handful of green onions and a tiny little bag of snow-white powder to an ancient-looking man who is steering along a boat-load of violet-coloured paste, which is in fact ground shrimps, an indispensable ingredient in Thai cooking.

And in among it all are the souvenirs and the shops on the riverbank selling colour film, postcards, Coke, straw hats and sunshades. The Floating Market on Klong Dao Kanong has gained a bad reputation because it has experienced an unprecedented commercial boom. But even if you are pressed for time, the early morning trip over the Mae Nam Chao Phraya (Menam River), through Thonburi, and up to the Floating Market is well worth while. The real attraction is the journey, which gives you a fine insight into life on the waterways of Thailand. These waterways reach incredible proportions: Thailand's rivers, canals, lakes and klongs are said to total over

3 million km in length, and form a much more closely knit system than the country's roads.

Any travel bureau will offer boat trips, and the hotels too will give you information and brochures about the best way to do things. If you hire a water-taxi be sure to agree the fare in advance, before casting off. One hour in a *hang yao* (one of the long narrow speedboats) is reasonably inexpensive. The famous river trip upstream from the Oriental Hotel, followed by a bus ride to Ayuthaya, and including lunch on board and the return journey by bus, is very good value and lasts all day.

The Snake Farm

Three snake pits contain hundreds of highly venomous reptiles. It is a sight to make your hair stand on end, especially at 11 am when it is feeding time for the cobras kept at this snake farm, which belongs to the Pasteur Institute (Saowapha Institute, Henri Dunant Road, near Chulalongkorn Hospital). The high point comes when wholly unperturbed workers horrify the spectators by climbing into the pits to 'milk' the deadly snakes. Of course, they tell you that even the most venomous snakes only attack humans if they themselves feel threatened; that does not alter the fact that many people are bitten in Thailand's rice-fields every year. The plus side of this is that the farmers can earn a little extra money by catching snakes.

The Pasteur Institute takes the yellowish venom, injects it into horses, and in this way can prepare the serum which is the only antidote for the deadly bite. Serum made here is distributed to hospitals all over Thailand.

Around Bangkok
Suan Sam Pran, the Rose Garden
(30 km from Bangkok)

The Rose Garden, Suan Sam Pran, is a kind of Siamese Disneyland: silk-weavers, silkworm farmers and potters, all assembled in a specially built bamboo village. In an open-air theatre cooled by two dozen propellors, the clichéd image of Thailand comes alive in front of your very eyes. There are swordfights and stick-fights, wedding dances and Thai boxing, cock-fights, bullfights, and elephants hauling great trunks of teak (daily, 3–4 pm).

Otherwise, the Rose Garden is a well-kept park with lots of flowers, beautiful trees, artificial ponds, fountains, a number of very good restaurants, two hotels and two swimming pools.

Ancient City
(Samuth Prakan, 33 km south-east of Bangkok)

In the same direction you will find 'Ancient City', an open-air museum with around sixty copies of traditional Siamese buildings. If you want to save yourself the long journey to the north to see the temple pyramid of Lamphun, or the seven towers of the Chiang Mai pagoda, then you will find they have built imitations of them here – and even a recon-

The Rose Garden, Bangkok

Snake Farm, Bangkok

struction of the Sri Sanphet Prasat, the great audience chamber from the heyday of Ayuthaya. And then there are souvenir shops, some reasonably priced imitations of valuable antiques, native animals roaming freely, folk-dances, and silk. (Open from 8 am–7 pm.)

The Crocodile Farm
(Pak Nam, 30 km south-east of Bangkok)
Thailand's native crocodiles are not enough for the crocodile farm, which breeds something over 20,000 giant creatures from Africa, Asia and South America. They are there less to provide flesh-tingling entertainment for tourists than to fill the frying pans of local restaurants and to meet the needs of the leather industry. The skins of these purpose-bred creatures are particularly highly prized. There are displays involving crocodiles and caymans, as well as other tropical beasts: tigers, leopards, snakes and elephants.

The Wat Pai Lom bird sanctuary
(on the right bank of the Menam, around 30 km from Bangkok)
Wat Pai Lom stands close to the town of *Pathum Thani* (itself well worth seeing as a settlement established by the Mon, who came to Thailand from Burma 2,000 years ago and have retained their own language). It is a typical riverside town, like hundreds of others in Thailand. Traffic, trade and industry are all focused on the Menam. Pathum Thani is famous for its rice noodles; you can watch them being produced, and of course try them for taste! It takes twenty minutes to reach Wat Pai Lom by motorboat (easily hired and not expensive, but agree the fare in advance). You see the attractions from a long way off: leafless trees dominated by huge cranes. The leaves have no chance at all against the birds' appetites. You can watch the colony from bamboo towers.

The rice plains

Across the Great Plain

The rice plains begin right on the fringes of Bangkok. Coconut palms and sugar-cane grow by the roadsides, but there is only one truly important crop here: rice. A system of dead-straight canals crosses the plain. Treadmills draw water up into the fields. All the way to the horizon you see a scene dominated by bent backs. Rice-working is all done with the back: relentless drudgery, with no shade and no great mechanical aids – people are still cheaper than technology. The yield per hectare is not terribly great, although modern methods could double it. Water buffaloes draw ploughs through the heavy mud. Thailand reveres the white elephant as its most sacred animal; it would be far more just if the water buffalo appeared on the national coat of arms, for without the water buffalo, the green granary surrounding Bangkok would not exist at all. The rice-growers' houses all look the same: made of wood, and stuck on stilts. This protects them from snakes and other undesirable creatures, and from the mud in the rainy season. The growers harvest just enough to live on. There is only one customer for their rice, and that is the government, which fixes prices. The splendid law of supply and demand only reaches the rice-farming system when world market prices fall. Thai workers earn just enough to feed themselves and to pay for a few of life's pleasures.

Nakhon Pathom

60 km to the west of Bangkok you will suddenly see a huge, shimmering gold finger pointing to the sky. It is, of course, a temple, but in this case a very special temple. Whenever a Thai king comes past, he is obliged to stop here and to offer candles and incense. The ashes of one of his forebears, King Rama VI, lie in a shrine here; but that is not the explanation. A holy relic of the true Buddha is preserved here. What is more, Buddha

Across the Great Plain

is said to have been here in person, to have rested and meditated here, and to have smiled his smile in the shade of a tree. All this was about 2,500 years ago. A place of prayer was inevitably created on such a hallowed site; it subsequently became dilapidated, was rebuilt, destroyed, restored, enlarged and embellished. What now stands there is 127 m high, and holds three records: as the tallest building in Thailand, resting on the oldest Buddhist place of worship, Phra Pathom Chedi is the tallest Buddhist structure in the world.

Hotel *Nakoru Inn*.

Phra Pathom Chedi

There are actually two buildings here: above the huge bell-shaped *stupa* in the Burmese style sits the slim, top-shaped spire of the chedi. This gleaming yellow-gold double tower is surrounded by a small walled square. A monastery of considerable proportions has developed — with all the additions that 2,000 years of pious labour have brought, and with each new generation trying to outdo the last. Both the circular balustrade running round the mighty stupa and the steps themselves can be negotiated. There is evidence in places of the ancient swastika motif. Precious statues of Buddha are kept in the inner sanctum. The mighty enclosing walls are broken at the four main points of the compass by *viharas*, large rooms given over to devotion. There is not a trace here of the sumptuous and rather overpowering decorative style found in Bangkok. The great building at Nakhon Pathom achieves its effect through the pure beauty of its proportions. However, it is beginning to show cracks, and there are birds' nests in some of the holes.

Origins

The legend surrounding the building of the first tower at Nakhon Pathom resembles that of the Oedipus drama: an astrologer had warned his king that he would be killed by his own son. The King immediately abandoned his newborn son. Of course, the child was taken in by charitable souls, and in time became a strong, heroic man who promptly overcame and killed the tyrannical king. Once inside his newly won palace, he fell in love with his own mother. After this dreadful secret had been revealed to him both by animals and by his stepmother, the son vowed to build a chedi to atone for his sins — and to build it 'as high as the wild doves fly'.

Kanchanaburi Pop. 15,000
(122 km north-west of Bangkok)
Kanchanaburi lies on the *Mekong River* and at the foot of the hills which form the not-too-distant border with Burma. One of the two tributaries of the Mekong, the *Khwae Noi*, has become world famous through the film *Bridge over the River Kwai*. (Day trips at the weekend start from Hua Lamphong Station, Bangkok, at 6.15 am.)

Hotel *Rama of River Kwai*.

The Bridge over the River Kwai

The true story took place on the edge of the town of Kanchanaburi. Pedestrians may cross the bridge; if a train comes thundering along, one can squeeze into one of the safe niches. The way to the bridge is easy to find, via road or boat. During the Second World War, the occupying Japanese sought to build a railway link running from Kanchanaburi to Burma, in order to safeguard their supply situation. They ordered tens of thousands of Allied prisoners of war to build the railway through the hellish jungle. It is said that 16,000 British, Australian and Dutch prisoners died during construction, as well as the quite unimaginable figure of 100,000 native Thais forced to labour for the Japanese. They starved, or died of thirst, exhaustion, yellow fever, cholera or malaria. The actual bridge over the River Kwai was destroyed by Allied bombs in 1945. The present bridge was built after the War – by the Japanese! The film of the same name was, incidentally, made in Sri Lanka.

Nam Tok

You can use the railway line built by the Japanese by way of war reparations to travel upstream to the terminus in Nam Tok. On your way you will see parts of Thailand which have remained relatively undeveloped. This stretch of line has a nickname which reminds the traveller of the horrors of the Second World War in the tropics: the 'Death Railway'.

Starting from Bangkok, there are one-, two-, or three-day rail excursions on offer. Part of the programme is a trip through the jungle as well as visits to isolated jungle settlements. There is also an opportunity to travel up the Kwai by boat, or to see a waterfall which is considered one of the great natural sights in Thailand – the 'Elephant Cataracts' (Erawan Falls, about 65 km from Kanchanaburi). If you can put the horrors of the River Kwai out of your mind, then the countryside between Kanchanaburi and the Burmese border just seems like a typical jungle. Of course, it has in part been expertly opened up to the tourist by means of raft trips, bungalows in the jungle, and facilities for fishing and trekking.

Bang Pa In

(60 km north of Bangkok)

The marvellously picturesque summer residence of Bang Pa In used to be the equivalent of Versailles for the Siamese kings. When nearby Ayuthaya was still the capital, they enjoyed visiting this large island in the Menam. A natural pond on the island was excavated to become 400 m long. When Ayuthaya declined, the royal summer residence slipped into oblivion.

However, the rulers of the new dynasty in Bangkok did remember Bang Pa In; this was in the second half of the 19th c., when active contacts had been made with Europe and Western forms and ideas were being eagerly adopted.

The Aisawan Thipya At Pavilion

In the middle of the miniature lake stands an elegant stilt building – a sort of concentrated version of everything that is Thai style. Romantics like to describe the Aisawan Thipya At Pavilion as 'Thailand's Taj Mahal', because the powerful and famous King Chulalongkorn (Rama V) had the filigree structure built as a memorial to his queen, who died here at the start of the 20th c. with three of their children when her boat overturned.

Varophat Phiman audience chamber

Behind the pavilion with its sad history the style suddenly changes. One thinks of Bavaria's Ludwig II, who had his weird castles built in styles from far away and long ago. The building in question is called Varophat Phiman and looks like a piece of European Rococo which flew here on a magic carpet. It actually served as an audience chamber. The little lake is framed by elements of post-Baroque landscape dominated by life-sized figures of gods. In front of you there fans out an intricate labyrinth of

Across the Great Plain 51

canals and bridges. There is also a neo-Gothic church; however, it is not a church, but a temple by the name of *Wat Nivet Dharmapravat*. The most expensive building in the castle grounds at Bang Pa In came as a present: the wealthy Bangkok Chinese dedicated the *Palace in the Peking Style* to King Chulalongkorn, and it is sprinkled with dragons, carvings, gold and statues, all imported from China. The Chinese Grand Emperor would have turned green with envy if he had ever visited the little King of Siam. But at that time, such excursions had not been thought of.

Bang Pa In is an extraordinary place: in the context of the rice-plains of Menam, it looks like a souvenir from a different planet.

Ayuthaya

(70 km north of Bangkok)

Ayuthaya (pronounced A-yút ya) is one of the most important names in Thai history. For over 400 years, from 1350 to 1767, it was the capital of Siam. Thirty-three kings ruled from here, almost four times as many as from the later upstart capital, Bangkok. Ambassa-

Ayuthaya

dors left Ayuthaya heading for Peking, Kyoto, Paris and Rome. This, the most splendid and the mightiest city in South-East Asia, was adorned with palaces, temples, avenues, massive walls, forts and ramparts. But none of it helped: in 1767 Siam's arch-enemies, the Bur-

Reclining Buddha, Ayuthaya

mese, conquered and destroyed the city after a siege lasting two years. All that remained was ruins. But even these battered remains of the old capital give evidence of their former regal grandeur. There are still some twenty major sights to see in Ayuthaya. The city is easily reached from Bangkok by rail, boat or bus.

A walk round Ayuthaya

Walking around the ruins of the city is like walking through Pompeii. There is no evidence here of the tinsel which smothers Bangkok's temples. Many of the structures have only their skeletons remaining, and are overgrown by the creeping edge of the jungle. Half-finished reinforced concrete columns surround the seated but now desecrated Buddha (his arms have been removed, but at least he has been freshly whitewashed). Some years ago, there were plans to build a modern roof to cover the site of the temple. Fortunately the authorities in Bangkok put a stop to this assault. Gifts are received from pious donors: imitations of other famous statues of Buddha stand among the 'colonnades'. On the city ramparts, there is a 600-year-old Buddha sitting in the gloom of the *Panan Choeng* temple. This gilded colossus, almost 20 m in height, survived the fall of Ayuthaya very manfully. He has long since been surrounded once again by crowds of pious visitors. Tiny temple dancing-girls follow the dull beat of the drums; clouds of blue incense swirl around the Great Seated One; and gold leaf glitters in the gentle draughts as the faithful stick it on to the body of the colossus.

Who was the benefactor behind this or that standing Buddha? When was a particular wall built? It doesn't matter. What counts here is the tragic silence of dead centuries. Ayuthaya's flawless majesty cannot be fathomed in the course of the bare hour allocated to tourist trips around the ancient capital.

The most important finds are now housed in Bangkok's National Museum. Ayuthaya has contributed more to Thailand's artistic heritage than any other Siamese city. Many of its kings were poets. Foreign travellers sent back rapturous reports concerning the city's wealth. In its heyday, Ayuthaya was so obsessed with its own magnificence that whole herds of white elephants were kept here.

What has remained untouched is Ayuthaya's remarkable location on a pleasingly symmetrical loop in the river. Nothing remains of the royal palace. It was made of wood.

Wat Phra Si Sanphet

Wat Phra Si Sanphet has suffered the ravages of the Burmese, of rainstorms, and simply of 200 years. Surfaces have been worn smooth or worn away. What remains is no more than the stumps of the *prangs*, little mountains of tiny bricks which you can now climb up. The reliquaries now lie empty, the high cornices are overgrown.

Wat Mahatat

The ruins are spread far and wide. Destruction took on new forms in the former Wat Mahatat: there is a whole army of mutilated Buddhas, and a number of collapsing towers just managing to remain standing and leaning like sick giants, crooked, on their last legs. One of them, though, did retain enough strength to preserve a treasure trove from the clutches of the plundering Burmese. In 1956, almost 200 years after the fall of Ayuthaya, archaeologists found this shrine full of relics, statues, written tablets, and jewellery made of pure gold.

Phu Khao Tong

This temple, popularly known as the 'Golden Hill Pagoda', was originally built by a Burmese king in the Burmese style. Once King Naresuan had managed to drive out the Burmese in 1574, he had the pagoda rebuilt in the Thai style. In 1956, following the restoration of Ayuthaya, a golden orb weighing 2.5 kg was placed on its spire.

Lopburi

(154 km north of Bangkok)

This was where King Narai received the ambassador sent by Louis XIV, some 300 years ago. In those days, Lopburi was the summer capital. The humid heat of Ayuthaya forced the court to seek the somewhat cooler conditions on the high plains of Korat, and so a royal palace had to be built there. The remains are still visible today. This was the era when the Greek Constantin Phaulkon served the King as a minister. Both the fortifications and the purely decorative buildings show a marked Western influence. At that stage in its history, Lopburi was already 1,000 years old.

Prang Sam Yod

The Prang Sam Yod temple, with its three towers, represents typical Khmer architecture. It was originally built as a Hindu shrine, and was only later rededicated to Buddha. The history of Thai art includes a category known as Lopburi style: some of the Buddha figures found here are outstanding examples of it.

Wat Prasri Ratana Mahatat

The dominant influence in Wat Prasri Ratana Mahatat is also that of the neighbouring Khmer. In the extensive complex south of the station are the remains of truly first-class buildings: even though the surfaces have been badly damaged, the unmistakable outlines of Khmer architecture are still intact.

The Reception House

The so-called 'Reception House' offers a splendid example of the generous attitude of the ancient kings of Thailand. King Narai had it specially built for the ambassador from Versailles, and then somewhat later had it extended to please his Greek adviser. The influence of European tastes is immediately apparent, even though the building is in ruins.

Saraburi

(108 km north of Bangkok)

Saraburi has a temple you would remember even if you did the rounds of all 20,000 wats in the kingdom of Thailand. It is majestic and austere, yet at the same time very serene and splendid. The golden shrine is enclosed by white balustrades. On top there is a light, airy cap of green and gold which tapers in a seemingly never-ending progression towards a delicate tip. Kept inside the shrine is a curious treasure: a footprint made by Buddha. It is of superhuman proportions: no ordinary mortal ever had feet that big!

Buddha's footprint

The finding of the footprint went like this: a stag, mortally wounded by a hunter, suddenly leapt out of the bushes completely healed. More than a little annoyed, the hunter could not even find a trace of blood; but he did find a puddle of water. The hunter drank a few drops – and suddenly felt reborn. He then noticed that the puddle was in the shape of a footprint. Although these wondrous events took place almost 2,000 years after Buddha's lifetime, the King was in no doubt that here was a footprint of the Enlightened One. Buddhist scholars confirmed his opinion, and the King promptly had a sumptuous shrine built over the footprint. The Burmese destroyed the shrine: the present illustrious temple came into being around 1800. Since then there has been a constant stream of pilgrims visiting the footprint of Buddha, which is 1.5 m long.

Nakhon Nayok

(135 km north-east of Bangkok)

This excursion takes you to some really impressive waterfalls. The road from *Hin Kong* leads through rice-fields, past busy canals full of boats, and past teams of water buffaloes; these frequently slow the journey, as Route 33 is narrow and bumpy anyway. Just before you reach the town, a side-road branches off towards *Wang Takrai*. Passing through a narrow, picturesque valley, you reach the *Nam Tok Salika* waterfalls. During the dry season there is, of course, very little water tumbling down the rocks. A second waterfall, *Nam Tok Nang Rong*, is located inside a well-tended park which was laid out by one of the royal princes and displays a good cross-section of Thai flora.

Exploring the romantic coast of the Gulf of Thailand

The coastal resorts on the Gulf of Thailand

The most famous beach in the country lies on the north-east coast of the Gulf of Thailand. Bangkok itself is only about half an hour from the sea, but you really have to travel almost 100 km down the coast to the south-east before you come to the proper beach resorts. The culprit is the Menam River, or more accurately the vast amounts of mud it dumps into the sea. You will have driven for an hour before you notice that the dark greyish-brown colour begins to dissipate and finally allows the natural colours of the Gulf of Thailand to emerge. There have been repeated attempts to construct bathing beaches close to the city, but they have all failed: the muddy waters of the Menam have always proved too powerful a force. So, if you are travelling in search of a good beach, don't bother stopping at *Samut Prakan* (there is not even a decent temple worth looking at). From here, *Sukhumvit Road*, Thailand's version of an east-coast motorway, aims straight south. The fertile alluvial plains are somewhat monotonous, but the lotus blossom forms a richly decorative element against the lush green carpet of the rice-fields. Fishermen haul huge nets along the canals; herons fly lazily past, seeming to wave to you with their swaying wings. One-armed windmills draw water up into the fields, and then return for a while to their slumbers. Between the road and the sea are the gurgling and slopping waters of a dense mangrove swamp. Now and again, you glimpse fields of gleaming white sea-salt. With no shade available, the burning heat shimmers all around.

Chonburi

90 km away, Chonburi lies in a fertile plain. There is a colossal Buddha here, remarkable more for its corpulence than for its artistic quality. This provincial capital is a typical small Thai town; it also provides an indication of the at first surprising fact that despite having 2,000 km of coastline the Thais have never really been a seafaring folk. It may be a stone's throw from the sea, but Chonburi has none of the characteristics of a coastal town. No wonder. Here — and this is true for considerable lengths of the Gulf coast — the water is so shallow as to be non-navigable for ships with a commercially viable draught.

Bang Saen

The 'Thai Riviera' starts around 100 km south of Bangkok, in Bang Saen. The water is still not quite as crystal clear as swimmers might have pictured it, but the evidence of tourism is unmistakable: bungalows, souvenir shops, kiosks, sunshades, promenades, luxury hotels overlooking the sea and the islands, and all sorts of watersports facilities. Although Bang Saen might seem a bit plain and simple when compared with some Italian, Spanish or French resorts, it still attracts a lot of holidaymakers during the hottest season.

The 18-hole golf course is among the most beautiful in Thailand.

Si Racha

An exotic little fishing village with coconut palms; it has no Western luxuries, and only simple accommodation. The major landmark on the bay is the temple standing on the Ko Loi rock, which is joined to the mainland by the harbour mole. The heat hovers over the beach as if generated by some great cosmic branding iron. Surprisingly, Si Racha boasts a Catholic bishop.

For decades, a narrow-gauge railway carried teak boles out of the jungle to Si Racha. You may just catch one of the last trips before this train rumbles out of service altogether. The elephants waiting at the jungle terminus handle the massively heavy hardwood trunks just as delicately as their more refined colleagues do in the open-air museums around Bangkok.

Ko Sichang

The island of Ko Sichang lies an hour away from the mainland by boat. This is where boats used to anchor when the depth of their draught prevented them from moving further towards Bangkok. Flat-bottomed boats would then reload their cargo just off Ko Sichang and ferry it across the extremely shallow coastal waters to the mouth of the river. The rocky island of Ko Sichang lost its significance when a clear passage to Bangkok was dredged, and only a little fishing village remains, together with a stone pyramid crowned with a simple *chedi*: King Chulalongkorn's summer residence was never quite completed.

Red Cliff Beach

About 20 km further on you will find Red Cliff Beach. It is not really a proper village: there are just a few bungalows equipped with the basic comforts and not attempting to be elegant. The place is designed for lazy days on the beach without those irritating ingredients found in the more restless holiday centres. Much quieter than Pattaya, and much less expensive.

Evening on the coast

Rock Cottages, Moonlight Beach, Palm Beach

The coastline is now becoming more jagged, with more bays. It is also much more built up. The names of these holiday villages indicate their origins: for years, American soldiers came here from Vietnam for rest and relaxation. Facilities are very simple.

Pattaya

(150 km from Bangkok; express coach service)

Pattaya also owes its now legendary growth to Americans taking leave from the various theatres of war in Indo-China. In the 1950s it was still a simple fishing village, but within ten years it had turned into Thailand's best-known and most lively holiday resort. New hotels are constantly being added, and there is an increasingly bustling atmosphere. Not that Pattaya's beach is particularly extensive, but there are many kilometres of beach on the nearby and easily accessible islands, where the swimming is really idyllic.

The resort follows the standard pattern: hotels and shops line a long main street which is open on one side to the sea. Pattaya has perhaps grown a little too rapidly: on Sundays it overflows with day-trippers from Bangkok. There is a lot of junk in the shops, but there is no doubting the vast range of pleasures

Pattaya beach

The coastal resorts on the Gulf of Thailand

Pattaya can offer.

The main street consists of a 5-km row of more than 100 hotels, restaurants, discos, bars and clubs. More than other resorts, Pattaya tends to produce divided opinions. It is loud and crowded, and a singles' paradise. You can get beer from the barrel everywhere, and even European cuisine. But it does offer watersports for everyone, from beginners to experts – diving, waterskiing, surfing, and the most daredevil watersport of all, parasailing. And on top of that it has those beautiful islands!

Pattaya does not have the finest sands in the world, and if you are looking for the best beaches and the clearest waters you will be better off bathing from the islands (see below).

Boat trips.

Diving, snorkelling.

Lots of bars, discos and nightclubs. The best bands in South-East Asia. Without putting too fine a point on it, the nightlife here is about as comprehensive as that on offer in Bangkok.

There are good trips up and down the Gulf coast starting from Pattaya. If you want to explore the surrounding area a little more, you can hire horses or even large Japanese motorbikes.

The offshore islands

The best thing about Pattaya is its nearby islands. A one-hour trip in a comfortable fishing boat – painted in gaudy carnival colours – and you climb out into what seems like the South Seas. Actually, you do climb out into the sea: the heavy motorboats have to anchor about 100 m off the beach, leaving laughing holidaymakers to wade through water which reaches a temperature of 35°C. The islands are called *Ko Lin*, *Ko Pin* and *Ko Sak*. Day excursions can be arranged, but the best thing is to hire your own fishing boat. They have room for between eight and ten people to sit quite comfortably, to lie under the awning, or to fish a beer or a lemonade out of the icebox, before swimming through the crystal-clear water to the dazzling white beaches. The islands are all crowned with dense green foliage and fringed with coral reefs; in the shade provided by woven palm fronds, crayfish and less familiar fish sizzle on the grill.

But Pattaya's dream islands can no longer claim to be untouched. There are open-air bars, and people selling shellfish, fans, rice-noodle soup, or mother-of-pearl spoons, and none of this fits our idea of a Robinson Crusoe island. But it doesn't really disturb the atmosphere, and it is a real pleasure to buy a few of the fabulous shellfish. Anyway, if you go a couple of bays further along, all of this ceases to exist, and you can spend the day stretching out on perfect sand, with a superb jungle behind you and marvellous bottle-green water in front of you. There is one drawback, though: it is very, very hot. The fishing boat snoozes, and its passengers fall asleep exhausted by the heat, by eating, by drinking beer from the icebox, and by diving into the lagoon. (To hire a roomy fishing boat for the day is not expensive. Drinks are extra, but cheap.)

Sattahip

Sattahip is Thailand's main naval base. However, don't expect to find huge ocean-going ships docked here. Political tensions in South-East Asia may indeed have led to a strengthening of the Thai navy – with US aid – but the result is hardly a gleaming armada. The fact that the Thais are not really sea-wolves, but tend to have a less than intimate relationship with the sea, may be deduced from their naval insignia: in the middle of its red, white, blue, white and red stripes there is not an anchor, or some other appropriate symbol of the sea, but an elephant!

Fishing harbour

More rewarding than the naval base is the fishing harbour. Here you can occasionally see men land one of the real terrors of the sea – a shark. The catch usually gives you a good idea of the wealth of fish the Gulf has to offer.

The little town is in a pretty location, with jungle-covered mountains overlooking the coast. (The passenger harbour is on the far side of the bay.)

A good beach.

Chong Samae San

The rather circuitous and complicated route to the coast makes it clear just how little the eastern corner of the Gulf has been opened up. Thailand can offer hundreds of seaside locations with islands, white beaches, and the guarantee of an authentic atmosphere free of any hubbub. Chong Samae San is a good example. The fishermen have already adapted to some extent to the tourist trade: for a decent reward they will ferry you out to the five islands lying just off the bay. These are mini-paradises looking like scenes from a Gauguin painting; dotted in the incredibly pure waters, they have lush vegetation and are fringed by snow-white sand. The scenery could easily convince you that the islands are still wholly untouched. But even this dream of an eternal holiday has one drawback: dangerous currents, which make it inadvisable to swim very far out into the deep-green waters of the Gulf.

Rayong

Rayong is almost bursting with boats. There is a strong smell of fish pervading the village – much stronger than it should be in a normal fishing village. The reason is that a selection of Thailand's famous thick fish pastes are prepared here. When you read about how the spicy Nam Pla paste is prepared, it does not at first sight seem terribly appetising. One of the sorts of fish found in great abundance in the Gulf is left to dry for six months and is treated in such a manner that it virtually decomposes. This is the source of the infernal stench. Spices are added to the unattractive fish mush until it becomes hot; it is then bottled, and becomes an absolutely indispensable and fundamental element in Thai cuisine. Nam Pla comes hot, hotter, and extremely hot, and is found in the Royal Palace, in the five-star hotels, and in every little shack in the country.

The idyllic island of Ko Samet lies just off the coast.

Ko Samet

Twenty years ago, even the real Thailand buffs did not know this name. But suddenly, Ko Samet was 'in': an elongated, narrow island – only 4 km long – lying in the Gulf of Thailand, reached from the fishing village of *Ban Phe*. The boat takes 45 minutes, and doesn't set off until it is full. Ten years ago, Ko Samet was, as you might expect, quiet and isolated. But that is all now a thing of the

The coastal resorts on the Gulf of Thailand

past. It is a national park, but is packed full, particularly at weekends. The splendid beaches still look like a scene from paradise, with their powdery sand whose high silica content makes the island glisten. Palm trees wave in the breeze, and surfboards flit across the eternal blue of the Gulf waters.

Prices for bungalows are low; international standards of luxury will not be found here. Fish, including crayfish, can be eaten absolutely fresh; and looking at the numerous coves and inlets you might think most South Seas postcards were photographed here. Ko Samet is to be recommended if you can get along without all the trinkets and tawdriness of Pattaya – and it is cheaper. There are a lot of young people here, and there are simple huts and bungalows. There are courses for windsurfers. There is even a fairly limited number of more comfortable bungalows. The restaurants are good, and they manage without posh décor.

If you are in a hurry, Ko Samet can be reached on a day trip from Pattaya (depart 7 am, return 6.30 pm).

Laem Mae Bhim

It is a bumpy country road which leads through the rubber-plantations to Laem Mae Bhim. Here, too, you can hire a fishing boat and be ferried out to the romantic islands, but this is a place where you really will find yourself wholly cut off from Western comforts. If you want to make yourself understood, you will have to rely on gestures and your ten fingers. Nobody understands a word of English here. Just 300 km from Bangkok, the illusion that you are on some desert isle in the South Seas is flawless.

Chanthaburi

(324 km south-east of Bangkok)
Chanthaburi lies in an area of great agricultural wealth: rubber, pepper, coconut palms and the stinking delicacy durian are all grown here. This wealthy provincial town is one of the few places in Thailand with a strong Christian element. There is a marked Chinese influence, too, which becomes clear when you first glance along the main business street with its bright array of goods for sale.

Beautiful sapphires and semiprecious stones are mined locally. You can even try your own luck at mining. One of the travel agencies offers trips to the gemstone mines, and armed with the appropriate tools you can drill and dig for your own gems. After that, it is 'finders keepers'!

From certain rocks they have discovered, archaeologists conclude that this is an extremely ancient settlement. You could not tell by looking at it; the Catholic cathedral dates from last century, and the houses would make a realistic tropical setting for one of Graham Greene's stories.

🛏 Simple but comfortable hotel rooms.

🍴 Good Chinese restaurants.

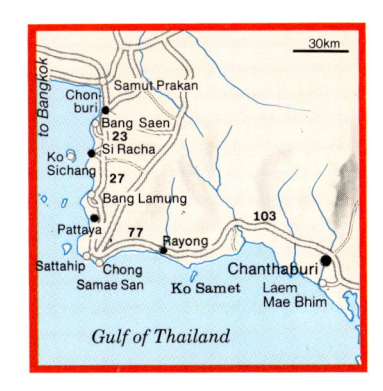

The north-east: a journey into the Khmer age

The north-east is the largest individual region in Thailand, and one third of the country's population lives in its sixteen provinces. The vast plains cannot compete with the exotic scenery around Bangkok, on the Gulf of Thailand, or in the north and the far south of the country. The sights and the significant towns are spread more thinly, and the whole region is poorer. Only *Pak Isan* is relatively densely populated. Nature was not quite as bountiful in the north-east as elsewhere: the soil is thinner, the rain is either very meagre or comes crashing down with catastrophic force, and the crops simply do not grow as well. This is why Yasothon Province holds its annual Rocket Festival. Praying to the weather-god Phraya Thaen for rain, the villagers fire their bamboo rockets skywards to the accompaniment of music and dancing. Only the right bank of the mighty Mekong and a few of the smaller valleys enjoy a lavish supply of water.

The lower standard of living in the north-east and the presence of communist neighbours in the shape of Laos and Kampuchea (formerly Cambodia) mean that the area is kept under close watch. The US-financed 'Friendship Highway' has provided the north-east with a fast-flowing main traffic artery, but its construction clearly also had a political motivation.

Access to the north-east is easy. After 150 km the highway – which is not really of motorway standard – climbs up on to the Korat Plateau. An apparently featureless landscape stretches out towards the horizon. During the summer rains it turns green, but then it rapidly turns to dust. Exotic elements become much sparser. However, if you are interested in obtaining a broad view of Indo-Chinese history, you are on the right trail. The remains of once imposing temples testify to the area's close connection with the neighbouring Khmer civilisation. In the middle of the dusty plain there is a quite sensational phenomenon: signs of a 7,000-year-old civilisation, whose discovery has tested the validity of all previous archaeological theories. Suddenly, it is not Mesopotamia which was the cradle of civilisation, nor China, but Siam – and specifically the village of Ban Chiang.

Khao Yai wildlife park

(Alt. 800 m; 2,000 sq km; 206 km from Bangkok)

Just before you reach Pat Chong, you arrive at the Khao Yai wildlife park. Here there are said to be tigers and bears, and even a wild elephant might suddenly emerge from the bush. But don't bet on it. It is only the monkeys who have learnt that contact with man can bring certain advantages, and they are all over the place. The lush, hilly landscape of the park is dominated by Khao Keo, the Green Mountain (1,350 m). The journey up to the park is rather tedious, but worth while, as is the small entrance fee.

With a genuine waterfall!

You can walk for miles through unspoilt jungle: excellent opportunities for jungle photographs.

Clean bungalows, planned and laid out by the Thai tourist authority. Demand is heavy, so book your accommodation from Bangkok.

There is a marvellously scenic 18-hole course.

The north-east: a journey into the Khmer age

Nakhon Ratchasima (Korat)
Pop. 50,000 approx.
(260 km north-east of Bangkok)
Nakhon Ratchasima is the official name for the provincial town of *Korat*, which for many centuries served as a base for the Thais in their struggles against the powerful Khmer. The only relics from the past are a few rather undramatic broken walls. Today, Korat is significant as a traffic junction, as the hub of a silk-producing region, and as an administrative centre. Not even professional tourist agencies seem to be able to dig up anything worth seeing in the town. Well, perhaps the monument to Thao Suranaree. She was a lady who stood up to an army sent from Laos. This motif frequently crops up in other places, and clearly has a most profound effect on the men of Thailand, who otherwise absolutely dominate their womenfolk.

Pimai
There are, however, many sights well worth seeing in the region surrounding Nakhon Ratchasima. Pimai lies 55 km to the north-east, acting as a kind of outpost to Angkor Wat, and giving a good idea of what the legendary Angkor is like. A single glance at the monumental ruins leaves you in no doubt: this was built by one of mankind's great civilisations – the Khmer, the forebears of the present population of neighbouring Cambodia. Pimai consists of a rectangular temple-complex; protected by ancient, massive walls, dominated by the steep face of its central tower, it is a classic Khmer monument. The temple was once surrounded by a town, 1,000 m by 550 m in area, which must have enjoyed a position of eminence as an outpost of the Khmer empire. Links with the hub of the entire empire – the incomparable Angkor – were close and complex. A road said to have been built around AD 1110 led directly from Angkor to ancient Pimai. In Pimai itself, no detail was left to chance: the complex betrays all the minute planning of an extraordinary architect. Even the restorations can be counted among the very best achievements of modern Thai preservation work. But above and beyond any scholarly appreciation of its many buildings, Pimai creates a strong impression, with its red sandstone walls standing out amid its pale greys and its weathered black, with its mountains of columns and cornices, and with its superb central tower. As long as political considerations put Angkor out of reach, Pimai can truly serve as a substitute.

Panom Wan
There is something worth seeing on the way to Pimai: Panom Wan, which lies 20 km north-east of Korat. One of the many footprints of Buddha is preserved here, in the middle of a Buddhist temple complex.

Phnom Rung and Muang Tam
Several of the 'medieval' (12th c.) Khmer ruins around Nakhon Ratchasima are rather difficult to reach. If you have a keen interest in art history, it is worth taking a taxi ride to *Phnom Rung*. The temple, sitting on top of a prominent hill, is another one with a Buddha footprint, and its ruins are particularly beautiful. *Muang Tam*, the 'lower town', lies on the plain and is surrounded by a well-preserved wall. There are two 11th c. Khmer temples to visit; they have splendid bas-reliefs and are set in romantic surroundings with attractive ponds.

Surin
(430 km north-east of Bangkok)
The silk town of Surin offers a spectacle which will quicken the pulse of those

The north-east: a journey into the Khmer age

Elephant drive, Surin

with video cameras. There is, though, one disadvantage – it only takes place once a year, in November. This is when some 200 elephants come together for the great *elephant drive*, a festival involving comic turns, incredible displays of skill, and a thunderous elephant race. There are also, of course, all the usual costumes and dances, along with the invocation of spirits, a parade, and at least one mock battle which shows that the elephant was the forerunner of the armoured vehicle. In the area surrounding Surin, elephants are trained for a life of work, though their numbers have very clearly dipped in recent decades. It is estimated that there are now a bare 100,000 left.

Wat Ra Ngeng and Wat Ban Prasat Yeu Nua

There are a number of ruined Khmer sites around Surin which are well worth seeing, particularly *Wat Ra Ngeng*: it offers five large Khmer towers with reliefs, in exotic surroundings. But foreign travellers will meet difficulties here, and can only counter them with stamina and a passion for Khmer sites. The problem is simply one of finding the place; most maps print only about a third of all town names in roman script, whilst villages are almost all in Thai script. Beyond the main tourist attractions, signposts are also written only in Thai. However, if you want to find the ruined temple of *Wat Ban Prasat Yeu Nua*, for example, you will have to travel along small country roads, dirt-tracks, and paths across fields, and even if you do hire a taxi, the driver will have difficulty locating out-of-the-way places because the signposts are so inadequate. Local directions frequently refer to trees or to bends in the river as landmarks. Nevertheless, if you take enough food with you, and are self-reliant by nature, you will find the task confronting you very rewarding.

Khao Phra Viharn

As long as Kampuchea remains closed to foreigners, you will have to make special arrangements to visit the magnificent temple of Khao Phra Viharn. It lies in the disputed border area which Thailand was forced to cede to Cambodia in 1963. Access is officially blocked, from both the Thai and the Kampuchean sides. At the moment the Thais will not normally permit tourists even to enter the border area, where there are camps brimming with Kampuchean refugees. If you do insist on trying, you should find out in Bangkok whether access really is going to be possible.

The cliff is vaguely reminiscent of the fortress of Masada in Israel. An 850-m stairway leads gently up the slope – a symbol of the long road to heaven, as understood by Hindus. In outline, the cliff itself looks like a supertanker. At the 'bow' end, the rock falls away almost vertically to the plain below. Just before you reach this high point you will find the shrine itself, in fact a complete holy city in compact form. The style is pure Khmer. Some of the buildings are virtual ruins, some are in first-class condition: houses of prayer, lotus towers, columns and stairways, all erected in the 11th c. and adorned with high-quality statues. You walk through a whole series of ornamental doorways and courtyards, past ponds, and below the austere splendour of cornices and gables. You sometimes wonder whether the Greeks or the Incas didn't have a hand in building all this. The two palaces, built around AD 1020, are of impressively regal proportions, and represent masterpieces of Khmer architecture. There is a panoramic view from the top of the cliff.

Ubon Ratchathani
(675 km north-east of Bangkok)
Ubon Ratchathani is one of those places that has two names: its ordinary workaday name is *Ubol*. The town lies on the *Mae Nam Mun* river, a tributary of the Mekong. There is no need to waste time looking for 'sights': Ubol is an important provincial town, a traffic junction, and the distribution centre for the regional economy. Its most interesting feature actually lies abroad, this time in Laos: the splendid Khmer temple of Wat Pu.

July/August: candle festival, with a float procession and dances.

A detour to Wat Pu

Once more, it is advisable to find out in Bangkok whether you will be allowed the opportunity of crossing the border. The Laotian embassy in Bangkok (193 Sathorn Road, tel. 2 86 00 10) can give you reliable information, and with luck your visitor's visa for Laos. Ask any travel agency in Bangkok, or your own courier, what it is like getting from Thailand to Laos at the moment! The best way to travel to Wat Pu is by taxi, and you had better be prepared for a whole day's excursion. Wat Pu enjoys an incomparable position on a terraced mountainside, and once again your breath will be taken away by the almost town-like proportions of this Khmer structure. Whereas Thai temples tend to be squeezed into a relatively small area of land, the Khmer classical period built temple complexes which resembled towns: they have their paved avenues and flights of stone steps, their systems of ceremonial courtyards, galleries and processional pathways, their palaces, and their lotus towers that are the most typical feature of Khmer architecture. Wat Pu was created around AD 1100 and is relatively well preserved. The shrine itself lies on the uppermost terrace, and houses a beautiful Buddha of quite respectable proportions which is accompanied by many, many smaller Buddhas. The view from the top over the Mekong plain and the encircling hills is something to be savoured.

The entire region to the south and east of Sisaket and Ubon Ratchathani is blessed with a wealth of Khmer sites. Some have been badly eroded by the weather, or are in ruins, but in many cases they are still impressive.

Khon Kaen

(230 km north of Nakhon Ratchasima)
Khon Kaen is the main town in the north-east. There is little to see, apart from a small museum, but the town is an important junction. The main routes to Vientiane, the capital of Laos, run through here. The town's university plays a vital role as a centre for education in the underprivileged north-east.

Phu Kradeung

A beautiful park offering long walks, waterfalls, and Buddhas. It is possible to spend the night in the forester's quarters near the peak of Phu Kradeung, but only with prior permission from the Forestry Department in Bangkok.

Loei

The economic centre of a fertile region. The Erawan Cave lies 19 km away.

Sakon Nakhon

A provincial centre, with only economic significance, but there are a number of beautiful spots in the surrounding countryside, as well as archaeological sites with relics from the Khmer period.

Udon Thani

The town is a supply centre and a military base.

Ban Chiang

About 30 km to the east of Udon Thani (Route 22) a side-road branches off to the hamlet of Ban Chiang. In the 1960s, bronze tools, ceramic shards and human skeletons were found here – which rather unsettled the archaeologists. This may well be the oldest settlement to be excavated anywhere in the world – older than all the sites between the Tigris and the Euphrates, and older than anything found in China. The bones and the artefacts found at Ban Chiang are 6,000 years old, perhaps even 8,000. Just in case anyone should offer you some coloured fragments or a rusty armband – don't touch! There would be huge penalties.

Nong Khai

Nong Khai is a border town on the Mekong, and forms the terminus for the railway line from Bangkok. The station lies outside the town. You would be well advised to find out in Bangkok whether you will be allowed to cross into Laos and visit the capital, Vientiane, situated just 16 km away.

The north-east: a journey into the Khmer age

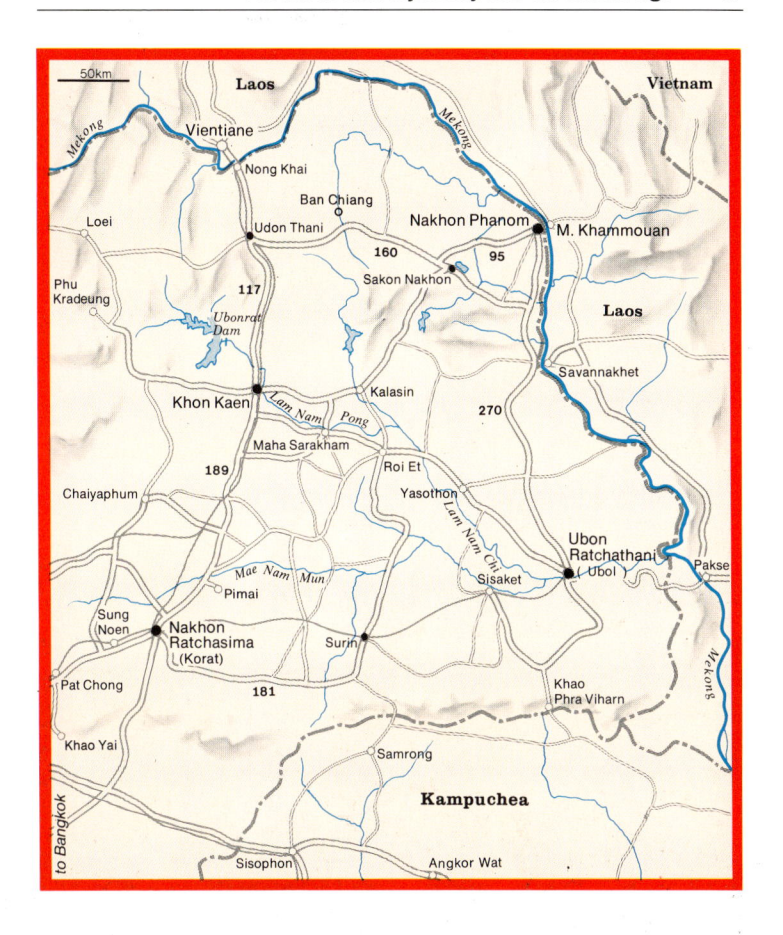

Ex Excursion to Laos

If the political situation should happen to allow you to take the bus trip over into the People's Republic of Laos, you will find the capital, Vientiane, has nothing very exciting to offer — at best, a superficial glimpse of life in communist Asia. But there is a royal palace, and the Wat Phrao Keo temple, now converted into a museum.

Sukhothai

Central Thailand

Sukhothai
(440 km north of Bangkok)

Sukhothai is the former capital, and lies almost half-way between the country's only two real cities, Bangkok in the south and Chiang Mai in the north. The inhabited part of Sukhothai is a peaceful little provincial town, and looks like a morose guard watching over the grave of an all-powerful ancestor. The ancient city lies dead and in ruins, the signs of its power smashed, plundered or decayed.

The golden age of Sukhothai was short lived, lasting little more than a century, from 1250 to 1379. In the later years its power waned so considerably that the kings of Sukhothai owed obedience to the ruler of the new capital, Ayuthaya. A great Buddha sits among shattered pillars, his smiling face blackened – a preservation problem for the archaeologists. The classical art of Thailand was once created around him, during the few years of Sukhothai's heyday, in the reign of Rama Khamheng. It was he who borrowed influences from China and India, from Ceylon and the Khmer empire, and tastefully blended them into a new style: the classic Sukhothai style of ancient Siam.

Ancient Sukhothai was protected by ramparts measuring 1,800 m by almost

Wat Mahatat, Sukhothai

1,400 m. Massive gates loomed over the entrance to the city. Twenty of the four dozen temples that used to stand in the city have already been excavated by archaeologists, as has one section of the royal quarters. The palace was burnt down some 600 years ago.

The shrine of *Wat Mahatat* used to stand in the middle of the walled city. You can see the stumps of its once splendid columns from afar, as well as the seated Buddha and the peak of the chedi. When you come closer, you can see a whole host of smaller chedis; there were once 185 of them. All around are signs of Khmer destructiveness. There is one small source of comfort for the pillaged city of Sukhothai: Wat Mahatat was twice copied – in Ayuthaya and in Bangkok (the Temple of the Emerald Buddha).

The sadness of the images will remain for ever: *Wat Si Sawai*, with its three remaining towers, and the elegant *Wat Sra Sri* on its little island in the lake. All that remains of *Wat Phra Pai Luang*, the Temple of the Great Wind, in the north of the city, is a dilapidated ruin. The *kilns* near Wat Phra Pai Luang, which were probably built and run by Chinese potters, offer a good insight into the technology available in the 13th c. Fine examples of what they made during the subsequent hundred years may be found in the *museum* at Sukhothai: jugs, bowls and plates, and also bricks and tiles used for building. In addition, the museum houses excellent finds from the ruined city itself. Once you have gained an overall picture of the collection you will be able to imagine just what Sukhothai must have looked like, and how it lived, and appreciate the extraordinary artistic sense which developed here in the short period when its culture flourished.

Si Satchana Lai

(30 km north of Sukhothai)

Si Satchana Lai, which lies near the River Yom, is another collection of ruins of major historical and cultural significance. Once again, it is the brick foundations of the chedis which have most stubbornly resisted destruction during 600 years in the tropics. The town used to have four temple complexes. There is just enough left of *Wat Chang Lom* and *Wat Chedi Chet Theo* to give some idea of how big they were. If you climb up *Wat Khao Suwan Kiri* hill and look back down over the town, you can see just how many ruins there are. *Wat Prasi Ratana Mahatat* lies 3 km to the east of the Si Satchana Lai ruins on a loop in the River Yom. It must once have been both a temple and a fortress, and its now useless remains, with their wealth of statues and stone carvings, lie in splendid isolation.

Phitsanulok

Phitsanulok was burnt to the ground in 1955, but rebuilt without too much difficulty. Spared this catastrophe was *Wat Mahatat* (the name occurs frequently in this region) with its Buddha which is famous throughout Thailand – *Phra Buddha Chinaraj*, a seated figure made of bronze. This particular Buddha is so highly revered in Thailand that there are imitations in many of the country's temples – even in the marble temple in Bangkok.

From Bangkok to Sukhothai

You can reach Sukhothai from Bangkok by rail or by road (Highway 1). Once you have left the concentration of sights at *Ayuthaya* and *Lopburi* behind you, the road heads straight for central Thailand – although that term does not cover a very clearly defined area.

Chai Nat

Chai Nat, though, is definitely part of central Thailand. Outside the town — which has no attractions to offer — the waters of the Menam build up behind the *Chai Nat Dam*. Finished in 1957, this dam plays an extremely important role in supplying water to Thailand's rice-growing plains. A complicated system of canals releases water from the dam and takes it via a network of channels to the distant rice-fields. Chai Nat is the starting-point for boat trips up the Menam, particularly to Wat Thanmanom.

Wat Thanmanom

From here you will have a splendid view over the broad and clearly luxuriantly fertile landscape alongside the great Menam River. The temple is not of exceptional interest. One of its Buddhas is said to exert a great influence over prophecies, however. The boat trip visiting places of interest for tourists takes you away from the main course of the river and into a network of tributaries and canals. A considerable proportion of the Thai population live in close contact with the waterways. The journey has no real dramatic moments (one hopes!) but does take you right to the heart of modern Thailand, even if it sometimes feels like a trip through a folk museum....

Nakhon Sawan Pop. 40,000

It is here that the Nan and Ping Rivers come together to form the Menam. The town bears a second name: *Paknam Pho*. Its location on the river makes it an important traffic junction.

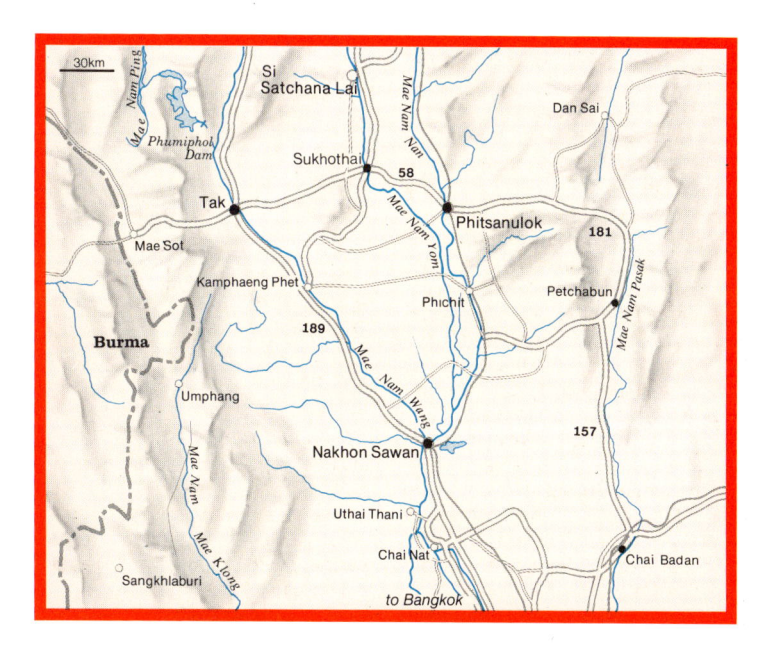

Kamphaeng Phet

Kamphaeng Phet was once a provincial capital of the Sukhothai kingdom. The ruins of *Wat Phra That* and *Wat Phra Keo* may not be breathtakingly beautiful, but they are worth pausing to look at. The flowing transitions from one style to another lend the buildings some art-historical interest. The *museum* houses finds from the town's brief heyday.

Mae Sot

The little out-of-the-way town of Mae Sot has remained wholly untouched by tourism. It lies 125 km west of Tak, and may be reached by an excellent new road which takes you close to villages occupied by three different tribes who clearly live in a very different way from their fellow countrymen. This area is absolutely virgin forest. Just before the road – which forms part of a planned Pan-Asian motorway – reaches the summit of a hill called *Doi Mussu*, a small surfaced track branches off to the right, and heads in turn through villages belonging to the *Lisu* and the *Musur* before arriving at the larger village of the *Meo* (Huong). All three are mountain tribes. If you want to photograph the people, you can reckon on having to make a small payment. If they do ask for cash, you should pay it and not turn tail, which would certainly cause offence. The Meo in particular are a headache for the Bangkok government. They are widespread throughout the west and the north of Thailand. The fact that there is a border does not prevent them undertaking frequent 'commercial' trips into Burma. They are in fact professional smugglers, and what is more, one of their main sources of income derives from growing poppies; opium is made from the poppies, and heroin from the opium.

The Meo women wear unmistakable long black skirts with knickerbockers and heavy silver jewellery, whose material value is far exceeded by the archaic beauty of its design. The mountain peoples are less open and forthcoming than are people in other parts of Thailand.

Once you get back on to the Mae Sot road, it goes past mighty teak forests and a chain of hills; then you reach Mae Sot itself, on the Burmese border. You may not cross the border without a visa.

Phumiphol Dam

About 60 km north of Tak lies Thailand's greatest technical marvel, which tends to be admired by the native population more than anybody else: the Yanhee Dam or Phumiphol Dam, the second biggest embankment dam in Asia, 486 m wide and 154 m high. Behind it accumulate the waters of the Ping, and its hydro-electric power-station provides electricity for Bangkok and thirty-seven provinces.

Boats can be hired on the 300 sq km of lake behind the dam.

The waters of the Ping cannot really compete with the crystal-clear waters of the Gulf of Thailand.

Northern village near Chiang Mai

Chiang Mai and the north

The north of Thailand has mountains as high as the clouds, and these mountains are covered with teak forests. Good-natured elephants carry the mighty pillar-like tree-trunks down to the river. During the hot season, from March to May, the days are dry and the nights cool. The King and Queen live in the north during this period. Crocodiles and leopards lie in wait for prey, and the last few tigers in Thailand stalk the endless jungles. The north has the friendliest people and the most beautiful girls. Thousands of artists work here, creating their works from teak and from old Indian silver rupees, or weaving the most gorgeous silks. The holiest and the most splendid temples are found in the north, and the tastiest fruit grows here, including many varieties which will not grow properly in the baking heat of the south. The north represents Thailand at its most exotic, and Chiang Mai is its greatest jewel.

Well, all this is true – but not absolutely true. It can be hotter in the north than in Bangkok (up to 42°C), although it is not as sultry, and the heat is thus more tolerable. The prices for northern wood-carvings and silverwork here are scarcely any lower than they are in the bazaars of Bangkok. When it comes to landscape, of course, the vast, crowded conurbation of Bangkok cannot compete with the north. No wonder: the five parallel mountain chains in northern Thailand are extensions of the Himalayas.

Everything is different in the north – well, almost everything. There are no beaches, it has highish mountains, little industry but a great deal of agriculture, jungles which remain impenetrable to this day, mountain villages still living in the Middle Ages, mountain trails hundreds of kilometres in length, raft trips through the primeval forest, and a simple life-style in simple dwellings. The difference becomes obvious as soon as you step out of your plane or bus and move a few kilometres into the country. Women in strange garb offer you all sorts of trinkets, jewellery and fruit. The mountain villages make you feel you are travelling in a different country: half a million non-Thais live here in almost 3,000 hut villages – immigrants from Tibet, China, Burma, Laos, Kampuchea and Vietnam.

If for once you really feel like getting away from all the usual luxuries of Western tourism, then head for the north of Thailand! Break away from the comforts of the holiday trade and have your own bamboo raft built at Tha Ton, right on the border with Burma; then take what will probably be the most adventurous trip of your life, floating down the upper course of the Nam Kok towards Chiang Rai, over the rapids and through the virgin jungle.

Getting to the north from Bangkok is easy. You can do the 750 km to Chiang Mai in the comfort of an overnight sleeper, or take one of the many daily buses which leave at 5.30 am, 1.30 pm and 7.30 pm. The lengthy bus trip is inexpensive. Thai Airways fly non-stop jets twice a day to the 'Pearl of the North'.

Chiang Mai Pop. 100,000
(750 km north of Bangkok)

Chiang Mai is the second biggest city in Thailand and the undisputed centre of the north. It is proud to be known as the most beautiful city in Thailand, a title which derives above all from its location at the foot of a 1,600-m-high chain of mountains overlooking the valley plain. During the rainy season, from May to the end of September, the humidity can at times become unpleasant, but is still well below the levels in Bangkok.

The founding of the city

Chiang Mai is a town of craftsmen and peasant farmers, an unusually peaceful place in the midst of verdant countryside. It is really more like a very large village. The people who live here are not descended from the Siamese but from their cousins the *Laotians*. They were already here when Thai hordes from the south of China began to infiltrate the area in the 9th c. Chiang Mai was founded in 1296. King Meng Rai gave the orders for building to commence, because his summer residence in Sarapi had been flooded so frequently. Searching for a dry area to build on, he was guided to this place by white deer and white mice. He acted immediately, believing he had been given a sign from heaven. However, the good omens were only of limited effect: the rulers of Chiang Mai died out at the end of the 15th c., and the royal residence was moved to Luang Prabang, since the late King's nearest relative was the King of Laos.

In later years, the warlike Burmese forced their way into Chiang Mai, remaining there for 200 years. By 1776 there was nobody left in the ancient capital. There followed a number of ultimately successful attempts to revive the town. The old town walls date from the early 1800s, and the splendour of its eighty temples was revived during the course of the 19th c. The buildings and the works of art date from the period when Chiang Mai was capital of the

Chiang Mai and the north 75

Elephants working, Chiang Mai

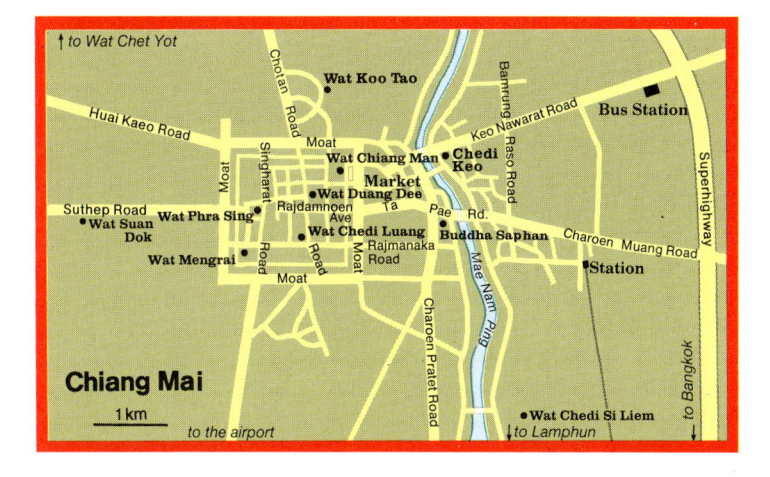

Chiang Mai

independent kingdom of Lanna Thai (Kingdom of a Million Rice-Fields).

A walk round the town

When you first stroll around, you might easily be disappointed: and a second look might not improve matters. Chiang Mai is a peasant village which happens to be full of temples and the treasures they offer, and is not really what we tend to imagine of a town with 100,000 inhabitants. Within the somewhat grid-like street pattern of the old rectangular town there are more peasant houses than shops and offices; agriculture remains the town's main source of income. It is only in recent years that multi-storey buildings have begun to appear. In 'winter', Chiang Mai is the only town in Thailand where you might just shiver with cold.

Chiang Mai has a *university* and an active Christian mission (Presbyterian), and is home to the famous *McKean Leprosarium*.

What remains of the ancient *city walls* scarcely suggests a military purpose. Children fish in the moat, and clearly catch quite a lot. You could never imagine these ramparts holding off an enemy who couldn't just as easily be sent packing with a few well-chosen words. Descriptions of Chiang Mai frequently talk of the 'Old Town'. Don't expect too much. This is a tropical town composed of timber and greenery, and only the 'sights' are made of more durable stone.

Foreigners may well be puzzled that Chiang Mai enjoys such legendary affection in the hearts of the southern Thais. Perhaps the reason is the presence of so many temples. Or the fact that you can wear a pullover in the evenings! Or perhaps it is the surroundings, with dark-green mountain jungles, wild orchids, and hazardous raft trips. It surely cannot have anything to do with the hustle and bustle in the town centre: Chiang Mai is just as noisy as Bangkok, and you sometimes have the unpleasant impression that every single motor-bike in eastern Asia is rattling through the town and spewing out its exhaust fumes.

Arts and crafts in Chiang Mai

The city has a fine reputation as a place to buy *handicrafts*, and produces a great deal of carving. Just like Europe in the Middle Ages, Chiang Mai has streets in which only *wood products* are made: plates, bowls, cutlery, elephants, and a million Buddhas, all the raw materials originating in the teak forests of the north. The *silversmiths* all congregate in another street. They have adapted their work to concentrate on what the tourists ask for most frequently. They all stock a wide selection of junk alongside jewellery of quite impeccably good taste, particularly the pieces created by nearby mountain tribes: armbands, necklaces and pendants, rings and earrings all in a uniquely severe style, almost archaic, decorated with austere lined patterns, and wholly divorced from the over-elaborate decorative style seen in Bangkok. (It is also very good value for money.) Chiang Mai's *antique-shops* are well worth visiting. Some of the shops employ a whole army of restorers, and part of the supply of gilded carvings comes from over the nearby border with Burma. Near Chiang Mai there is an *umbrella-makers' village*, as well as numerous *silk-shops* and *silk-weavers*. The local *lacquerwork*, in the Chinese idiom, is a matter of taste. The *dolls in local costume*, made by the mountain tribes, are famous throughout Thailand.

In general terms it may be said that

Umbrella-painting, Chiang Mai

prices are very reasonable.

The part of the city calling itself *Old Chiang Mai* is in fact new, and is a shopping centre for souvenirs. Again, the local mountain tribes are represented by their costumes and their various products, but also by their dancers. It is, of course, a purely commercial matter for them, but you can't necessarily tell that from your holiday slides. And among the mass of souvenirs you can always find here and there a marvellously made piece which is very cheap. The region's *ceramics* have been famous for centuries.

Chiang Mai's Night Bazaar, in Chang Klan Road, is a popular place for tourists to shop.

Song Kran, the Thai New Year festival, April 13th–15th. A procession where Buddhas are carried from their various temples and sprinkled with water in a purification rite. *Lamyai Harvest Festival*, in June. This region is Thailand's main producer of the lamyai fruit, also known as the 'devil's eye'. *Loy*

Wood-carving, Chiang Mai

Chiang Mai and the north

Krathong, at the beginning of November, is another major procession.

Luxury hotels: *Hyatt Orchid, Chiang Inn, Rincome, Poy Luang*. Middle category: *President, Garnet*.

Temples of Chiang Mai

You will only enjoy Chiang Mai to the full if you are truly mad about temples. If you aren't, you should stick to the seven major ones; you will only have missed about seventy-five!

Wat Phra Singh

Wat Phra Singh is virtually a 'bishopric': the primate of the local monastic management board lives here. The chedi dates from 1345; the highly venerated figure of the *Seated Buddha* arrived a little later, from Ceylon. The Buddha has been stolen, and carried around Siam and copied, so frequently that it is no longer possible to say with any certainty whether the present figure is the original. The *library*, with its excellent figurines, is a real gem.

Wat Mengrai

This temple may look brand new, gleaming in all the colours of the rainbow, but it was originally founded in 1298. The most recent renovation turned it into an ice-skating rink.

Wat Chedi Luang

Located in the city centre, this temple was inaugurated in 1411 and destroyed by an earthquake around 150 years later, although the interesting lower section survived. It forms an impressive example of northern Thai architecture. The *prayer hall* is guarded by huge divine serpents and peacocks. Holy relics are preserved in the many small surviving chedis. The famous Emerald Buddha, Thailand's most venerated holy object, stood in Wat Chedi Luang for eighty-five years. Nowadays it is exhibited in Bangkok. At the entrance to the temple there is a little house standing under a rubber-tree: Lak Muang, the city's protecting spirit, lives here.

Wat Chiang Man

The building of Wat Chiang Man, the oldest temple in the city, was started in 1297 under Chiang Mai's founder King Mengrai. He lived here until the city was completed, and he also died in Wat Chiang Man; there are hieroglyphics recording the event, but nobody can decipher them properly. The most valuable Buddhas in the city – one is made wholly from semiprecious jewels – are found in this temple. One particularly venerated Buddha image, allegedly 2,000 years old – a small stone figure in an unusual posture – will be shown to you by the abbot on request.

Wat Suan Dok

Clustered around the great, worn chedi of Wat Suan Dok is a veritable forest of seventy dwarf chedis. Their contrasting colours produce superb visual effects. In the *holy shrine* itself, a beautiful Buddha dating from 1462 sits on a throne surrounded by his disciples. Packs of long-legged dogs trot through the royal urnfield. Occasionally, the simple houses used by the monks seem to be decorated in saffron yellow; but that is just a result of the monks hanging out their freshly washed robes to dry.

Wat Kao Tue

In the chedi there is a bronze statue of Buddha, 500 years old. It is one of the largest and most beautiful in the entire country.

Wat Koo Tao

This temple is of interest primarily because of the way it came into being. King Tilokaj of Chiang Mai sent architects to India to study the famous chedi of Buddha Gaya. When they returned in 1477 they built a copy in Chiang Mai.

Phu Bing summer residence

There is a modern highway winding its way from the plains towards Phu Bing, the summer residence of the Thai King and Queen. It was built when the British Queen came here to visit them. You cannot visit the castle – a contemporary structure with some Thai elements added on – when the royal couple are in residence. If you are out of luck, you will have to make do with talking to the guards; that *is* allowed.

If you do get in, you can walk through the royal gardens, look at the royal living-quarters and guest quarters, peep in through one of the cellar windows, and see flowers blossoming which do not really belong in the tropics: the King's 200 gardeners grow plants from Europe.

Ex Excursions to the mountains

Chiang Mai also constitutes a base for excursions into the northern mountains. A two- or three-day journey will take you to the Burmese border, and includes a boat trip along the Nam Mae Kok from Fang to the burgeoning little town of *Chiang Rai*.

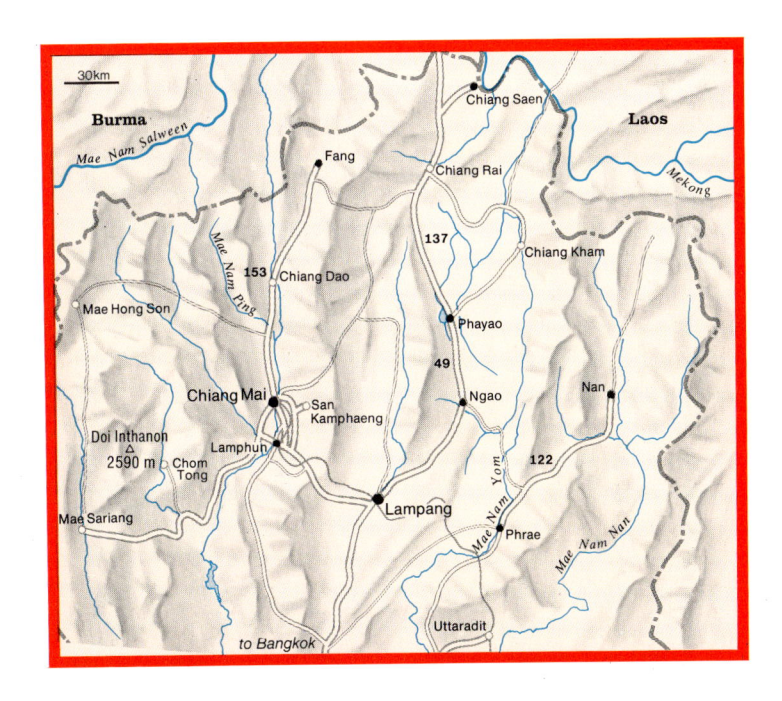

Meo children

Mountain tribe villages
This is the region where you will find villages belonging to the Meo and other tribes. Their standard of living clearly falls short of that enjoyed even by the poor rice-farmers. The *Meo* are not a smiling people. If you visit one of their villages, they will demand (and insist they get) a fee for being photographed. These proud mountain tribes are so openly disdainful of the state authorities that they publicly ignore the ban on producing opium. In a village not far from the royal summer residence of Phu Bing there are signposts pointing you towards the vast poppy-fields, whilst in the souvenir shops they sell postcards showing opened poppy heads and elderly women smoking opium pipes. The government battle against drugs is only slowly beginning to have an effect. Nowadays the main growing-areas are confined to Afghanistan, Pakistan, Laos and Burma. The Meo travel to their tribal brothers on the far side of the Burmese border without bothering about passports and visas. If anything is worth smuggling, they will smuggle it. The Meo look rather like the Chinese stereotypes in Hollywood films, often wearing little black caps, and red sashes wrapped around their dark cotton suits. Like the Thais, they stem from China; they have been active opium-growers since time immemorial, and are devotees of a complex form of spirit worship.

There are around 70,000 *Karens* living in the northern provinces. They have little contact with the tourist trade, but permit visits by arrangement. The 20,000 *Lisu* are closely related to the *Akha*, and both tribes only arrived in Thailand at the beginning of the 20th c. They are peasant farmers, and they too grow opium, despite government efforts to promote the subsidised growing of tea and maize.

For years the 15,000 *Yao* produced nothing but opium, but now they are being converted to growing rice and keeping cattle.

The mountain monastery at Doi Suthep
The best view of Chiang Mai is to be had from the mountain monastery of Doi Suthep, 700 m above the plain and 1,084 m above sea-level. A good-quality highway leads almost to the monastery door, but before you enter the golden sanctuary you will have to climb still further, up 290 steps flanked on either side by intertwining seven-headed snakes. Wat Phra Suthep is a splendid and fascinating monastery. Even the most seasoned temple-visitor will find something worth looking at: the filigree parasols on all four corners of the chedi,

Woman of the Yao tribe

Wat Phrathat Haripunchai

This is one of the most beautiful temples in the entire country, and when you consider there are some 20,000 to compete against, that is no small claim. At its heart stands a pale gold chedi, with the gold parasols typical of the northern style, two imposing statues of Buddha, ornately carved doors finished in gold leaf, frescos, flocks of birds, groups of young monks, naïve folk art and the refined, stylised art of an advanced civilisation, worked in brick, teak, plaster, stone, gold and mirror glass. There is no hint of the museum here; it remains just as alive as it was 1,100 years ago.

Wat Chama Devi *(Wat Kukut)*

If you have decided to see just one the statue of the white elephant, the bronze bells, the long covered walks with their paintings depicting the life of Buddha, and the golden chedi itself, which looks like a giant teakettle.

Lamphun Pop. 12,000
(26 km from Chiang Mai)

Lamphun (or Lampoon), the modern centre of the weaving industry, was formerly known as *Haripunchai*, and for 600 years, during the reigns of forty-nine successive kings, was the capital of its own kingdom. It was not a very large kingdom, but goes down in history as one of the many *Mon states* which stood out for a considerable period of time against the superior strength of the Thai and the Khmer.

Rice and garlic are grown here, and the lamyai plantations are a major source of income for the town.

Wat Phrathat Haripunchai

more temple, you ought to visit Wat Chama Devi, also known as Wat Kukut. Most of the temple buildings are of no great importance, but at its core stands a steep, five-storeyed pyramid with sixty niches for statues: a first-class example of late Mon architecture. Legend has it that the pyramid underwent repairs as early as 1218, centuries after the ashes of Queen Chama Devi were interred here.

Pasang

The weaving-village of Pasang lies just beyond Lamphun. There are said to be some 2,000 looms in the village. The main-street shops offer the tourist a wide assortment of materials and clothes.

Lampang

Lampang looks something like an ancient town: it still has carriages drawn by ponies, and the atmosphere is still strongly Chinese. The influence of nearby Burma — and of the numerous incursions by the Burmese — may be seen in the town's temples. Little remains of the ancient defences. Lampang, like Lamphun, was once the capital of its own kingdom. Twenty snow-white chedis are to be found in *Wat Chedi Sao*.

The Ngao elephant school

If you turn left some 54 km along the Lampang–Ngao road, you will reach the elephant school. From June to February, on weekday mornings, you can watch the young elephants being trained.

Chiang Saen

Chiang Saen, probably the oldest Thai capital outside China, lies on the Mekong. Nowadays it is more of a vil-

Wat Chedi Sao, Lampang

Akha village near Chiang Rai

lage than a town. It shares the bitter fate of many border towns throughout the world – of being the first to be destroyed. The temple ruins on the fringe of Chiang Saen testify to this fact. Accommodation is in the simple Chinese style. It is possible to take raft trips along the mighty Mekong.

Nan Pop. 15,000

Nan, another former royal capital near the Burmese border, is unfortunately so far off the beaten track that hardly any tourists visit its remarkably beautiful temples. Apart from these, there is a real rarity to be seen in the local council offices: a black elephant tusk.

Chom Tong
(58 km from Chiang Mai)

There are two natural marvels near Chom Tong: the *Mae Klang waterfall*, which plunges down some 100 m in several stages, and the *Sacred Cave of Borichinda*; both are favourite haunts of the northern Thais. The *Doi Inthanon National Park*, with the 2,590-m-high *Doi Inthanon* – the highest mountain in Thailand – lies 40 km further on.

Chiang Dao
(77 km from Chiang Mai)

The caves at Chiang Dao are extensive, and are said to stretch for 10 km. You can hire lamps and will pass numerous Buddhas on your way into the darkness.

Chiang Rai
(940 km from Bangkok)

This is a good starting-point for those adventurous treks and raft trips. There are a number of temples worth looking at in the town, which forms an important traffic intersection near the borders with Burma and Laos, not far from the infamous 'Golden Triangle'. A remarkably large security force is stationed here by the government, in order to keep track of the opium trade. Even if you cannot get as far as the mountain peoples' villages – usually accessible only by difficult routes through the mountain forests – you will at least see members of a number of tribes in Chiang Rai marketplace.

Phuket

The long tail: the south of Thailand

Thailand's long tail stretches southwards for some 1,500 km, as far as equatorial Malaysia. There is a great deal of rain here, particularly between October and December. The wind blowing from the sea searches out every nook and cranny: nowhere on the Malaccan Peninsula is far from the coastline, whether it is the shores of the Gulf of Thailand on the one side or of the Indian Ocean on the other. An uninterrupted 'spine' runs from north to south through the peninsula, consisting of densely green jungle-clad mountains. All previous plans to break through the narrow finger of land and build a canal – in order to shorten the sea route to eastern Asia by some days – have foundered on the presence of these mountains. During the 1980s, connections to the distant southern tip of Thailand, with all its treasures, were noticeably improved. The express train from Bangkok to Penang spends thirty-six hours travelling through unspoilt tropical scenery, the road from the capital to the southern border of Thailand is tarmac all the way, and the south is even reachable by a scheduled air service. For long stretches the twin coasts remain virtually untouched paradises. But things are slowly changing. Hua Hin saw the beginnings of change, Phuket followed, and so did Songkhla.

Thailand's southern seas are the coming place, particularly the numerous islands

The long tail: the south of Thailand

which all look like perfect tropical idylls: snowy white beaches fringed by the shade of dark-green palms, and a turquoise-blue sea lapping a shoreline still untouched by the hustle and bustle of the tourist trade. The further south you go, the less rice there is to see; it is replaced by rubber-plantations. Temples gradually become a rarer sight as mosques become more widespread. The south is characterised by its breathtaking natural beauty, with incomparable views of sea and mountains.

Ratchaburi
(100 km south-west of Bangkok)
Ratchaburi once lay by the sea, but is now 30 km from the Gulf, and the Mae Klong River is still continuing to lay down its alluvial deposits. This is the region where they make the heavy pitchers in which Thai households store their water.

Petchaburi
(150 km south-west of Bangkok)
Petchaburi is an ancient trading place and a site where diamonds were once found: its name in fact means 'Diamond Town'. There are a dozen beautiful temples – such as *Wat Mahatat* on the left bank of the river, *Wat Nakhorn Kiri* with its marvellous views, and *Wat Kum Pang* in the Khmer style – worth including in a walk round the town.

The resort of Cha-Am, much loved by the Thais, lies 66 km to the south.

Hua Hin
(200 km south-west of Bangkok)
This was the first real resort on the Gulf of Thailand; it is more refined than *nouveau riche* Pattaya, and its beaches and waters are cleaner. If the royal couple want a holiday, they go to their palace at *Klai Kang Won*. The oldish Railway Hotel is considered one of the most beautiful places to stay in all Thailand; despite being so famous, it also has reasonably priced bungalows. The Thais see Hua Hin as *the* place to go for a beach holiday. The sands, for example, are a lot more extensive than in the much newer resort of Pattaya. The notable buildings in Hua Hin are not temples, but the lavish millionaires' villas – of the kind also found in neighbouring Cha-Am. There is also a famous 18-hole golf course.

The best food is found at the open-air stalls in the marketplace. It costs very little, and there is fresh fish, oysters, shrimps and freshly boiled vegetables.

Hotels: *Railway, Sai-Lom, Regent Cha-Am* (high class; about 20 km north of Hua Hin).

Wat Mahatat, Petchaburi

Prachuap Khiri Khan
(320 km from Bangkok)
This is a splendid location on the Gulf, and has no tourist trade – and thus, of course, no Western-style luxuries: the ideal spot for a simple beach holiday in the tropics. (Don't be put off by the nearby military air base.) Close by there are waterfalls, and you are surrounded by jungle, monkeys, fields of pineapples, and mountains up to 1,000 m high. There are also three small islands with isolated bays and caves.

Chumphon
(500 km from Bangkok)
At Chumphon the main road suddenly turns west to cross the *Kra Isthmus*, the narrowest spot on this long, thin finger of land, a bare 50 km wide. The isthmus has become well known for those periodically revived plans to blast a canal through the peninsula at this point, in order to spare ships the detour around the Straits of Malacca.

Hotel *Sri Chumphon* (with air-conditioning).

Ex A detour to the west coast

Kraburi
Kraburi, from which the isthmus derives its name, has little of interest to offer: only the huge *Tham Prakhayang* cave is worth getting out to see. The scenery is like something out of a geography textbook: everything you ever imagined by way of a tropical wilderness is concentrated here (though with any luck you won't see a cobra!). It is all jungle, mangroves and islands.

Ranong
At Ranong the main road reaches the Indian Ocean. The houses look remarkably European.

Hotels: *Thara, Sin Ranong, Asia* (all air-conditioned).

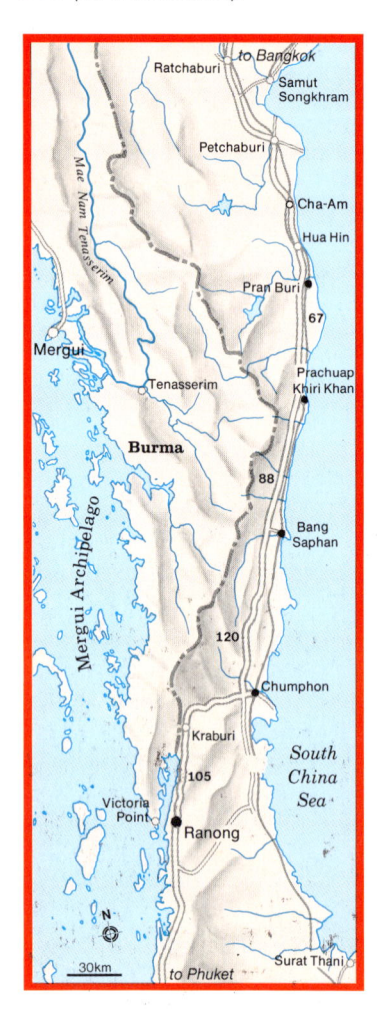

The island of Phuket

Within twenty years, the attractions of Phuket have made it one of the main tourist goals in the whole of South-East Asia. It enjoys a very favourable location, and is only 70 minutes away from Bangkok by jet. Sixteen splendid bays seem to embrace the sea; the hinterland is well-tended, fertile country; there are no temples you really have to visit; the best hotels on the island are on a par with top international competition, and even the more modest accommodation is spotless and inexpensive. The island – at 600 sq km the largest in Thailand – is clustered around by an archipelago of smaller islands ideal for day trips with their broad bays and their barbecue facilities. Fish and lobsters are caught fresh for you, and the service is first class.

The island of Phuket is wealthy, and its wealth actually predates the point when holidaymakers started landing at its little airport: Phuket has the most productive tin-mines in Thailand. You can see them from the road – tall structures which from a distance look like roller-coasters. The ore-bearing shale is washed with pressurised water. Phuket's roads are all brand new. There is building taking place all over the interior of the island. Pineapples ripen in the sun. This bountiful island also produces wolfram, rubber and coconuts.

Twenty years ago Phuket was only for those in the know. Now, next to Pattaya, it is the largest tourist centre in Thailand, with an annual 400,000 or more tourists, and it has been organised right down to the very last detail.

The capital, Phuket

The capital of Phuket is likewise called Phuket, and is a little tropical town built in a curious Portuguese-Chinese blend

Phuket

The long tail: the south of Thailand

Tapu Mount, Phang Nga

of colonial styles. The streets are straight, and are lined by two-storeyed shops and offices with ornately decorated façades. The shops are mainly Chinese, and crammed full of goods in an unpretentious but tidy fashion. Most shops are located on Rasda Road and Talang Road, or near the big hotels. As well as the customary souvenirs you might also get in Bangkok, Phuket has a particular speciality: pearls from the local pearl farms, all manner of shells, and handicrafts fashioned from mother-of-pearl.

The governor wears a peaked cap, but wears no tie when he is sitting with friends in a bar. Piles of the stinking durian fruit give off their clouds of evil-smelling aroma. In the evenings, numerous young girls with their hair newly done and with freshly ironed clothes sit in brightly lit conservatories. The scene may look to you like an adult evening class, but in fact you are seeing one of the town's fifteen brothels.

The temperature hardly drops at night, and the weather is particularly exhausting during the May–October monsoon season. The waters of the Indian Ocean are very warm. There are no important temples to visit.

Numerous small restaurants offer Thai and Chinese specialities. Seafood is particularly recommended.

The bay of Phang Nga
(90 km from Phuket)
There is an excursion from Phuket to some quite breathtaking scenery worthy of the South Seas: the journey takes you back to the mainland, to the neighbouring province of Phang Nga. Here you climb into a motorboat. The sea in these parts is crowded with rocky islets. Made of limestone, many shoot straight up like a bishop's mitre. The renowned rocky island of Thum Lod embraces a deep tunnel-like fissure; your boat will go through this, and then there will open up a labyrinth of lagoons, with mangroves hugging the shore, monkeys screeching, and sea-eagles circling overhead. The little stilt village of Ko Panyee is anchored just in front of one of the green-shrouded headlands.

Ko Panyee
Visitors will feel as if they are stepping back into the Stone Age. The fishermen and their wives and happy children are by now used to being visited by the white strangers with big noses. There is one massive stilt building here – the school. The teacher wears a tie, which is probably the only tie in the whole of Phang Nga province. If the amiable teacher at Ko Panyee catches hold of you, it is quite possible that you will have to sing a song for his children. They will laugh themselves silly and clap as if you were Callas.

Ping Kun
The real jewel among all these rocky islets is Ping Kun. The Ping Kun rock stands with one foot in the water, rises up to display a broad pair of shoulders, and is crowned with trees. This striking formation is surrounded as far as the eye can see by other islands. An incomparable sight.

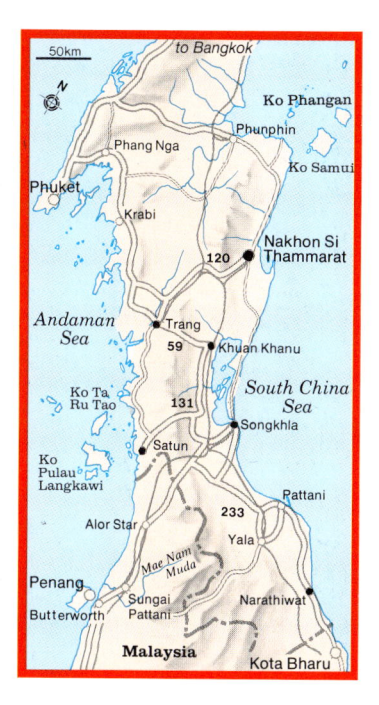

The stalactites at Suwanakhuha
The Suwanakhuha cave lies about 7 km from Phang Nga. Numerous statues of Buddha stand among the stalactites and stalagmites.

Krabi
The nearest reasonably large place on the mainland is called Krabi. Nothing much goes on here, but you cannot ignore the splendid scenery of the Malaccan Peninsula. There are a number of unmarked side-roads leading to the sea and to some enchanting and wholly deserted beaches. Krabi is a bus-

Buddha statue, Ko Samui

tling little fishing harbour and a starting-point for boat trips to the bay of Phuket. Once again, the amazing shapes and sizes of the rocky outcrops provide incomparable scenery.

Ko Samui

Ko Samui is the third largest and perhaps the most beautiful of all the islands in the country. If you are fed up with the office, or the factory, or any sort of urban life, and want to get away once and for all to your desert island, then Ko Samui is the place for you. But the journey here requires some patience. Jets cannot (yet) land on the island's tiny airstrip, and it is only recently that there has been a service from Bangkok in a comfortable propellor-driven plane. The more stylish way to arrive is in the express boat which hurtles across from Ban Don (near Surattani). This takes three hours. (The big ferries take 6 hours to make the crossing.)

But perhaps you should hurry: there is already an asphalt road encircling the island. There are ambitious plans to open Ko Samui right up, and that will probably be the end of this little idyll. The 240 sq km of island will begin to fill up with infrastructural amenities. Until then, the fronds of a million palms will continue to wave in the breeze, and the evening entertainment will remain within the realms of the tolerable; there are amazingly cheap bungalows available, and meals and the abundant selection of tropical fruits ripening on the fertile island are inexpensive. The main pastime is of course watersports, at all levels. One of the great pleasures is hiring a boat (with navigator) and going out to the smaller islands.

Nakhon Si Thammarat

On the east coast of the peninsula, somewhat off the main road, lies Nakhon Si Thammarat. This is an ancient town, at least 1,200 years old. The ever-eager Portuguese established a trading post here as early as 1516. Numerous temples point to the former wealth of this once vital port, particularly *Wat Mahatat*, with its 77-m-high reliquary tower dominating the huge monastic complex. Near the town there are mountains rising to 1,700 m, and long beaches – although the town itself, also known by its Malayan name of *Ligor*, no longer lies on the coast. Here you will find the best shadow-play puppets in Thailand, as well as silverware, jewellery, and an exotic market.

Hotels: *Neramita, Siam, Thai* (all air-conditioned).

Songkhla Pop. 40,000

The population of Songkhla is mainly Muslim Malays. This is a historic place with the sea to its east and a lake to its west. Even the King comes here. The location is superb, and Songkhla has managed to retain its old charm. There are long beaches and pretty houses: it all looks like a film set. Songkhla is particularly popular with holidaymakers from Malaysia. There are flights to and from Bangkok.

Hotels: *Samila, Choke Dee.*

The southern tip of Thailand

The further south you travel, the more obvious it is how far you are from Bangkok and how close to Malaysia. The scenery remains superb. Your trip should include the following three places.

Pattani

Especially worth seeing in Pattani are the Chinese temple, the mosque, and the Rajah's palace dating from the days when the town was independent and autonomous.

Yala

Yala is a busy commercial town with a predominantly Chinese population. It lies in extraordinarily fertile surroundings. Nearby there is a Buddha cave to be visited.

Narathiwat

(1,530 km from Bangkok)
Narathiwat may be reached from Bangkok by a rather irregular shipping service.

It has a beautiful beach.

Useful things to know

Before you go

The climate and when to travel

Thailand's tropical monsoon climate, with its three changes of prevailing wind every year, produces three seasons: the hot season from February to May, with average temperatures of over 30°C; the rainy season from June to September or October; and the 'cool' season from November to February, with average temperatures of 25°C and the lowest levels of humidity. This period, which corresponds to a European summer, sees the north-east monsoon bring relatively cool, dry air from China. An exception is along the east coast of the Malaccan Peninsula, where there is high rainfall even during the winter months. Between May and September, the wind switches round and the south-west monsoon brings hot and humid air from the Indian Ocean, and with it the rainy season. This does not mean that it rains all day, but that when it does rain the rain is very heavy. With the exception of the far north, the climate is hot and humid everywhere, even at night.

Shopping for your trip

Basically, you can wait until Bangkok to buy everything you need for a few weeks' holiday. Film is dearer in Thailand, though, and the films you will be offered by itinerant traders are often useless because they have been stored under the wrong conditions.

Entry formalities

Visitors from most Western nations require a passport valid for at least six months, and a 15-day non-extendable transit visa obtainable on arrival. If you are staying longer, or are coming on business, you will need a different visa which you apply for at the appropriate Thai consulate or embassy (see page 94). On arrival in Thailand, foreign visitors must be able to prove that they possess cash or travellers' cheques totalling a specified amount, which should be checked with your travel agent before departure. If you cross a land border into Thailand, you will find your appearance being scrutinised. If you look scruffy, you might be turned back.

Customs regulations

You are forbidden to bring in any form of narcotics or written pornographic material. If you wish to bring in any weapon you will have to obtain a permit from the police authorities. You may bring in duty free: one camera, one video camera, five films and three video films, binoculars, cigarettes or tobacco for your personal consumption (maximum 200, or 250 g), and a litre of wine or spirits. Gold jewellery has to be declared on a special form; valuables may be recorded in your passport.

If you wish to take antiques out of the country you will have to apply for the appropriate permit. Tourists who ignore this regulation can reckon on receiving a large fine and having the articles confiscated. To apply for the export permit you must show the authorities both the object itself and two photographs of it. It may take up to three weeks to process your application. The responsible authorities in Bangkok are: the *Fine Art Department*, Na Phrahathu Road, or the *Ministry of Commerce*, Sanamchai Road. No matter what assurances the antiques dealer might give you, get your permit from the Fine Art Department. Buddha statues and Ban Chiang pottery may not be taken out of the country.

Vaccination

Yellow fever inoculation is only compulsory if you have been through a known infectious area, or one where there is an epidemic, less than ten days before your arrival. Tropical doctors do recommend, however, that you should have injections against cholera, typhus, tetanus, polio and hepatitis, and take precautions against malaria.

Your medical kit

Medical provision is adequate in all the tourist centres. Any of the big hotels can quickly summon a doctor familiar with all the usual health problems affecting tourists. If you are inclined to suffer from stomach upsets, you should take appropriate preparations with you. Western-standard hospitals are available in Bangkok and Chiang Mai.

During your stay
Currency and changing money

The Thai currency is the baht (1 baht = 100 satang). Since rates of exchange fluctuate, they should be checked in the national press or at banks. You can change money in your hotel, at the bank, or at a private money exchange, which frequently offers the best rates. You are recommended to take dollar bills, as these are accepted in even the most out-of-the-way places. Euro-cheques will be exchanged by the following banks on a limited basis – normally three per month: the *Thai Farmers Bank* in Bangkok and Chiang Mai, and the *Asia Trust Bank* in Pattaya. International credit cards are seldom accepted by small shops and inns, especially in the countryside. Foreign currency with a value equivalent to $10,000 can be brought in and taken out without being declared.

Buses

There are two types of bus: scheduled non-air-conditioned buses with their narrow seats, which are really exhausting for longer journeys, and scheduled air-conditioned buses run by the national bus company or private tour operators: these have toilets, and on long-distance trips offer you free drinks. They are a bit more expensive, but generally travel without taking any long stops.

The bus network is comprehensive and reliable. The bus is the primary means of transport in Thailand, and offers very good value for money. There are about 280 regular routes, and you will be able to reach even the smallest village – well, almost! Timetables are printed in Thai, so you will need to get your information from a travel agent. Buses are quicker than trains in Thailand, though they are a little riskier: the drivers are somewhat daredevil.

Trains

There are three classes on the trains, of which first and second class are in line with European standards. Usually only first class is air-conditioned. The trains are punctual and reliable. You are recommended to book if you are travelling on popular routes or at peak times. Despite the numerous supplements to be paid for sleepers, express trains, and private compartments, travelling by train is still very inexpensive. (Information and reservations: tel. 02/2 23 70 10 or 2 23 37 62.) This public transport system is comprehensive and well developed. It embraces some 4,400 km of track.

Car hire

Cars are available for hire from a number of companies in Bangkok. The cost varies according to type, and depends to some extent on the firm involved, but is very reasonable. Petrol is not included. Addresses and contacts are available from Thai Tourist Offices or from your hotel reception desk. However, you are not advised to drive yourself around: the traffic on the streets is chaotic, and on top of that most Thai drivers do not even have third-party insurance.

Taxis

There are standard taxis, and then there are the more expensive and more comfortable hotel taxis (see page 36). Whenever you take a taxi, agree the fare in advance! There is a stand for public taxis in the international terminal of Bangkok's *Don Muang* airport. The trip to the city centre is not expensive. For shorter trips you can take the little three-wheeler tuk-tuks, but again be sure to agree the fare in advance. Most of the drivers speak very little English.

Post and telephone

Bangkok's main post-office stands on New Road (tel. 2 33 10 50). There are sub-post-offices in all the major hotels.

Since 1985 it has been possible to dial direct to thirty-two countries.

Tips

Tourist hotels and restaurants reckon on a 10% service charge. They also expect, but do not insist on, a 5–10% tip. It is deemed impolite to give 2 baht or less: it would be better to give nothing at all. Taxi-drivers have no claim to a tip, but are only too keen to accept one, particularly if they have helped you carry your cases. Hairdressers, porters and tourist guides expect a tip. At the airport there is a fixed rate of 10 baht for each piece of luggage; at the station it is 3–5 baht. It is important that you give the tip in a friendly manner.

Opening hours

Public offices are open from Monday to Friday 8.30 am–4.30 pm; in Bangkok, it is 8.30 or 9 am–noon and then 1–3.30 pm. Most shops are open from Monday to Saturday 10 am–7 pm. Smaller shops may even stay open 8 am–9 pm. Department stores in shopping centres are often open at the weekend. Apart from when you are in major stores and the better-quality shops, it is normal to haggle over prices.

Electricity

Voltage: 220V, 50Hz.

Newspapers

There are daily English-language newspapers in Bangkok – the *Bangkok Post* and the *Bangkok World*.

Important addresses

Diplomatic offices

British Embassy
Wireless Road
Bangkok; tel. 252 7161/9

US Embassy
95 Wireless Road
Bangkok; tel. 252 5040/9

Canadian Embassy
11th Floor, Boonmitr Building
138 Silom Road
Bangkok; tel. 234 1561/8

Australian Embassy
37 Sathorn Tai Road
Bangkok; tel. 286 0411

New Zealand
93 Wireless Road
Bangkok; tel. 251 8165

Useful things to know

Tourist information

In Thailand
Tourism Authority of Thailand (TAT): 2 Rajdamnoen Nok Avenue, Bangkok. Open daily: 8.30 am–4.30 pm. A very useful address; the TAT gives printed information about every region in the country, together with the latest lists of recommended restaurants throughout Thailand.

In UK
TAT
9 Stafford Court
London W1X 3FE; tel. 071 499 7670

In US
TAT
5 World Trade Ctr
Suite 2449
New York
NY 10048; tel. 434 20433

Index

Ancient City   46f.
Ayuthaya   16, 17, **51ff.**

Ban Chiang   66
Bang Pa In   50
Bang Saen   56
Bangkok   3, 7, 9, 16, 18, 20, 22, 26, 27, **32ff.**
  Chinatown   43f.
  Democracy Monument   43
  Golden Mount   42
  Grand Palace   37
  Jim Thompson's Thai House   11, 43
  Klongs   44ff.
  National Museum   43
  Snake Farm   46
  Suan Pakkad Palace   43
  Wat Arun   42
  Wat Benchama Bopitr   42
  Wat Phra Keo   37ff.
  Wat Po   40ff.
  Wat Suthat   42
  Wat Trimitr   42

Cha-Am   85
Chai Nat   71
Chanthaburi   61
Chiang Dao   83
Chiang Mai   20, 27, **74ff.**
  Phu Bing   79
  Wat Chedi Luang   78
  Wat Chiang Man   78
  Wat Kao Tue   78
  Wat Koo Tao   79
  Wat Mengrai   78
  Wat Phra Singh   78
  Wat Suan Dok   78
Chiang Rai   79, **83**
Chiang Saen   82f.
Chom Tong   83
Chonburi   56
Chong Samae San   60
Chumphon   86
Crocodile Farm   47

Doi Suthep (see Chiang Mai)

Elephant school (Ngao)   82

Gulf of Thailand   55ff.

Hua Hin   85

Kamphaeng Phet   72
Kanchanaburi   49
Khao Phra Viharn   65
Khao Yai   62
Khon Kaen   66
Ko Lin (see Pattaya)
Ko Panyee   89
Ko Pin (see Pattaya)
Ko Sak (see Pattaya)
Ko Samet   60f.
Ko Samui   90f.
Ko Sichang   56
Krabi   89f.
Kraburi   86

Laem Mae Bhim   61
Lampang   82
Lamphun   81
Loei   66
Lopburi   53f.

Mae Sot   72
Moonlight Beach   57
Muang Tam   63

Nakhon Nayok   54
Nakhon Pathom   48f.
Nakhon Ratchasima (Korat)   63
Nakhon Sawan   71

Index

Nakhon Si Thammarat 91
Nam Tok 50
Nan 83
Narathiwat 91
Nong Khai 66

Palm Beach 57
Panom Wan (see Pimai)
Pasang 82
Pathum Thani 47
Pattani 91
Pattaya 6, 21, **57ff.**
Petchaburi 85
Phang Nga (see Phuket)
Phitsanulok 70
Phnom Rung 63
Phu Kradeung 66
Phuket 21, **87f.**
Phumiphol Dam 72
Pimai 63
Ping Kun 89
Prachuap Khiri Khan 86

Ranong 86
Ratchaburi 85
Rayong 60
Red Cliff Beach 56
River Kwai 49f.
Rock Cottages 57

Sakon Nakhon 66
Saraburi 14, 20, **54**
Sattahip 59f.
Si Racha 56
Si Satchana Lai 70
Songkhla 91
Suan Sam Pran 46
Sukhothai 16, 17, **69f.**
Surin 20, **63f.**
Suwanakhuha 89

Thonburi 18

Ubon Ratchathani 65
Udon Thani 66

Wat Ban Prasat Yeu Nua (see Surin)
Wat Pai Lom 47
Wat Pu 65f.
Wat Ra Ngeng (see Surin)
Wat Thanmanom 71

Yala 91

Original German text: Friedrich Müller. Translation: Robert Aylett in association with First Edition Translations Ltd, Cambridge
Series editor, English edition: Jane Rolph

© Verlag Robert Pfützner GmbH, München. Original German edition

© Jarrold Publishing, Norwich, Great Britain 1/91. English language edition worldwide

Published in the US and Canada by Hunter Publishing, Inc.,
300 Raritan Center Parkway, Edison NJ 08818

Illustrations: J. Allan Cash Ltd pages 36, 47, 73, 84, 90; James Davis Travel Photography pages 1, 68, 80, 88; D. Dickins page 19; P. Van Eenbergen pages 12, 48; Eyecatchers pages 22, 75; M. Jarrold cover and pages 15, 28, 29, 41, 42, 81 (top), 83; R. Johnson pages 3, 13; Tourism Authority of Thailand pages 21, 24, 25 (left), 26, 43, 77, 82, 87; World Pictures pages 4, 10 (left), 32, 52, 58, 64, 69, 77.

The publishers have made every endeavour to ensure the accuracy of this publication but can accept no responsibility for any errors or omissions. They would, however, appreciate notification of any inaccuracies to correct future editions.

Printed in Italy

ISBN 0–7117–0485–6